SAVING OUR
LAST NERVE

SAVING OUR LAST NERVE

THE BLACK WOMAN'S PATH TO MENTAL HEALTH

MARILYN MARTIN, M.D., M.P.H.
WITH MARK MOSS

HILTON PUBLISHING COMPANY
ROSCOE, ILLINOIS

Acknowledgment

Support for this project was provided by an unrestricted grant
from Eli Lilly & Company. The author and publisher would like to
thank Eli-Lilly, Inc. for its support.

Published by Hilton Publishing Company, Inc.
PO Box 737, Roscoe, IL 61073
815-885-1070

www.hiltonpub.com

Publisher's Cataloging-in-Publication
(Provided by Quality Books, Inc.)

Martin, Marilyn, 1957–
    Saving our last nerve : mental health tactics for the Black woman /
by Marilyn Martin. — 1st ed.
    p. cm.
    Includes bibliographical references and index.
    ISBN 0-9675258-7-X

    1. African American women—Mental Health. I. Title.

RC451.4.M58M37 2002   616.89′008996073
                                    QB102-200379

Printed and bound in the United States of America

In Memory of

Rebecca Lucretia Martin

Virginia "Betty" Guinty

Dr. Maxie Collier

Dr. Jean Spurlock

My own life's journey has been enriched by the people who have journeyed with me. I extend my gratitude to them, my family, friends, colleagues, ministers, and patients.

In addition, I thank the Teaching, Supervising, and Training Analysts of the Baltimore-Washington Institute for Psychoanalysis, Inc.

And, finally, thanks to Tyler Alexander and Tina Rebecca.

Saving Our Last Nerve

CONTENTS

INTRODUCTION 1

CHAPTER ONE
THE RUIN OF A NATION BEGINS IN THE HOMES
OF ITS PEOPLE 7
Strong Families Build Strong Societies

CHAPTER TWO
THE SHEEP ARE AS GOOD AS THE PASTURE
IN WHICH THEY GRAZE 23
Patterns of Coping, for Better and for Worse

CHAPTER THREE
ONE DOES NOT CROSS THE RIVER WITHOUT
GETTING WET 39
How to Recognize and Cope with Stress Common to the Black
American Women

CHAPTER FOUR
THE MOUTH IS SMILING, BUT IS THE HEART? 59
Common Mental Illnesses in Black Women
The Necessity of Facing One's Illness
How to Find Treatment for Mental Illness

CHAPTER FIVE
MAKING PREPARATIONS DOES NOT SPOIL THE TRIP 85
Creating a Life Management Plan

CHAPTER SIX
ANTICIPATE THE GOOD SO YOU MAY ENJOY IT 103
The Path to Recovery and Healthy Self-Esteem

CHAPTER SEVEN
WHEN SPIDER WEBS UNITE, THEY CAN TIE
UP A LION 117
Negotiating the Mental Health System

CHAPTER EIGHT
A SINGLE BRACELET DOES NOT JINGLE 139
Love, Intimacy, and Relationships

CHAPTER NINE
THERE IS NO MEDICINE TO CURE HATRED 157
Prejudice and Our Mental Health

CHAPTER TEN
WHEN ONE IS IN TROUBLE, ONE REMEMBERS GOD 169
The Role of Spirituality in Mental Health

CHAPTER ELEVEN
ONLY THE WATER IS SPILT; THE CALABASH IS
NOT BROKEN 179
The Future is Ours to Create

NOTES 197

SELECT BIBLIOGRAPHY 203

INDEX 207

INTRODUCTION

"You're getting on my last nerve!"

You have screamed those words, and so have your friends and relatives. They are words born of complete frustration, and it's a safe bet you can't recall how many times you've shouted them. But you do remember that those times were frustrating, sometimes regrettable moments that came close to breaking the back of restraint.

You had nearly lost that last nerve.

Suddenly, you needed more information on that Biblical character named Job, and you went searching.

But what you were actually looking for was peace of mind. It's that simple.

Pinpointing your final goal is the easy part. Reaching it, saving that last nerve, requires struggle by both spirit and mind. Simplifying that journey is what this book is all about. Hard journeys are always a little easier when you don't have to make them alone. My book tells Black women what they need to know to maintain the mental balance necessary for living in today's demanding and stressful world.

Saving Your Last Nerve was conceived in a workshop I presented at Sisterspace and Books, a Black women's bookstore in Washington, DC. The participants were women who were tired of trying to be Superwomen. They were stressed, depressed, and determined to get out of the mess that was stealing their joy. They rejected the notion, sadly all too common in the Black community, that it is shameful and weak to seek guidance on life's path.

I want to share with you how these women learned to live with what they had to live with and make the very best of it. That's what it is to cope. That's what it is not to get worn down to your last nerve. To reach that balance, each of these women had to reach deep inside herself and get in touch with what she was really feeling, wanting, fearing, and suffering.

We all know how easy it is to get lost. When people get in their own way, by making the same mistakes over and over, it is often because in childhood they learned a coping pattern that they've not been able to change. Sometimes the problem is caused by overprotective parents, who, for example, want to teach their child to ride a bike but are afraid to let her peddle for herself. A steady diet of such overprotection can help create a woman who is incapable of realizing her potential later in life. The child who isn't given the opportunity to fall and get back up will be fearful of taking chances when she becomes an adult.

Our ability to interact with others, emotionally, is also determined by how our parents dealt with us. If we had affectionate and affirming guardians, then we learned how to express ourselves and our needs were met. But if we had parents who were cold or not receptive to our needs, we learned to stifle our feelings. And as adults we do the same, so we end up failing in our relationships.

In this book, I invite you to look inside in order to discover the strength that's deep within you. The reward I promise is the knowledge and resources you need to keep your mental balance and to raise your children in such a way that they'll grow up emotionally happy and strong. So I will speak to two generations, present and to come.

I've mentioned that Black Americans usually avoid turning to others for help until it is nearly too late. That general principle certainly applies to the specific case of mental health. True, there was a time—happily, a time past—when mental illness was used as an excuse to shackle those of us who listened to a different drummer. The result was that many Black women are afraid of the mental health care industry, and buckling under pressures we could have handled if we'd had a little help. That's why we need to open ourselves up to the many resources that can improve our emotional lives.

We need to open ourselves up to the many resources that can improve our emotional lives.

Thanks to the sacrifices of people who came before us, we, as Black American women, have now been allowed to participate in the American Dream. More of us are filling offices and climbing ladders. But these new opportunities don't relieve us of our traditional obligations. We're still having children, caring for parents, and maintaining homes. We continue to provide for those who depend on us. With all these responsibilities, we're caught in the speeded-up pace of existence everyone seems to be living these days. What it boils down to is that we carry quite a load, and if we don't balance it just right, we're likely to experience mental health problems that can also become physical problems.

Depression is an example of one of those problems that affects our functioning. It is one of the mental disorders spawned by our problematic childhoods and heightened by the stress of our present lives, among other causes. Depression affects a person's physical and mental ability to function, and is the number one reason that people don't go to work; the tally in lost productivity is immense.

Depression can also have a deadly human cost in physical terms. The World Health Organization forecasts that, by the year 2020, depression will be second only to heart disease as a cause of premature death and disability. Depression is one of the major causes of the 30,000 suicides that occur in the United States each year, and, according to the Centers for Disease Control (CDC), is also a major cause, particularly in young Black American men, of the 20,000 homicides committed annually in the United States.[1]

Finally, depression and anxiety threaten the very fabric of our community, contributing to substance abuse and under-achievement in school.

But it doesn't have to be that way. Depression is a highly treatable disease. In order to get treatment, you have to know when you need it and where to go. *Saving Our Last Nerve* will show you the door to the pantry of your emotional health. This book will also help you take stock of what is already on the shelves and what you need.

This book teaches you how to take your mental health inventory by explaining and showing:

- why people feel and behave as they do
- why some people keep falling into behavior patterns that hurt them
- how to change those harmful patterns
- how to raise your children to be mentally healthy and strong

Along the way, you'll also learn:

- the names and symptoms of mental disorders and the drugs that can treat them
- the wide range of available treatments
- when it's time to go beyond this book and seek professional help from your primary care physician and the specialists he or she recommends

You will also be asked to participate in exercises (enlightening little workouts) that, if you do them conscientiously, can be essential tools for *Saving Your Last Nerve*.

In writing this book, I have drawn upon two invaluable resources. The first resource is the wisdom of our ancestors. Each chapter is titled by an African proverb, which continues to speak out to us over the generations. The second resource is the many patients that have been courageous enough to share their stories. While it was necessary to disguise these patients to honor their trust, their struggles are common to the many Black American women I have worked with in my practice.

CHAPTER ONE
THE RUIN OF A NATION BEGINS IN THE HOMES OF ITS PEOPLE

Strong Families Build Strong Societies

Brenda

Brenda had been with the company for twenty-two years but now her boss had given her an ultimatum: *Get help, or pack up and go home.* She couldn't really blame him. For each of the past seven years, she'd used her sick and vacation days before half of the year was over–and then continued to miss work. She was out so many days her paycheck suffered, and she could barely pay her bills. She'd also run out of excuses with her boss, who was now losing business because she was not there to process orders. Her relatives, friends, and church members had long since stopped calling. They were tired of hearing her problems and just wanted her to get on with her life. On her end, she didn't call them because she was afraid they would ask for the money they'd lent her.

The first time Brenda came to my office was the first time

she acknowledged to herself that she had a real problem –not just that she might lose her job but that she was no longer someone who could be counted upon at work and at home.

"Honestly," she told me, "I don't know why I'm acting this way. I'm destroying my life. Can you help me?"

I told her I could, and that's what I am also telling you.

So let's begin. Your thoughts and actions, along with your genes, determine your health and well-being. They also determine whether you, as a Black woman, can effectively manage day to day struggles. We have a history of beating the odds, of throwing away the baggage of poverty and racism and moving on. Today many of us can punch the air in jubilation at having triumphed over adversity.

Sadly, too many of our sisters have gotten left behind because they have lacked the mental health necessary to negotiate life's obstacles. According to *Minorities and Mental Health: A Report of the Surgeon General*, released in 2000, Black American women suffer from higher rates of depression, anxiety disorder, and phobia than Black American men. While the overall rates of mental illness among Black Americans are similar to those of White Americans, Blacks are over-represented in "high need" populations–people in prisons, psychiatric hospitals, inner cities, and rural areas; and people who are homeless. The report states that these groups aren't adequately represented in major studies; if they were, "higher rates of mental illness among African Americans might be detected."[1]

Mental health, in essence, means

- shedding age-old habits that possibly cause stress, and replacing them with behaviors that reduce stress

• acknowledging and addressing biological and environ-
mental risk factors that may contribute to difficulties

To unload the baggage of our lives, we have to get help. But
before we are ready to seek help, we first must get over the
shame we experience from our "weaknesses," and overcome
the other barriers that prevent us from visiting mental health
providers or using resources, such as this book, that address
mental health concerns.

Frederick Douglass said, "It is easier to build strong children than to repair broken men." Adults who are treated for
emotional problems are often struggling with scars from
childhood. A famous study showed that this shouldn't sur-
prise us: parents who are verbally abusive, carry on arguments
in front of their children, or provide poor supervision and
inconsistent rules to those children, are more likely to have
children who were anxious and depressed, and who raised children of their own who develop anxiety.[2] As early as their teens,
these children of abusive parents are more likely to become
substance abusers. In short, they're more likely to get derailed
before starting their journey.

Other studies have looked at parents who are depressed
and found that depression interferes with good parenting. A
depressed mother will devote little time to the needs of her
child. While breast feeding, for example, a mother suffering
from depression may be so distracted that she won't make eye
contact with her child, which disrupts the bonding process.
The mother is experiencing so much difficulty handling
what's going on in her life that she can't appropriately attend
to her own child's needs.

What we learn in childhood strongly influences our adult behavior. Our inner child often dictates our adult life. You can see that in the ordinary ways we do things. Most of us tie our shoes the same way we did as children, and if we were asked to do it differently, we'd have problems. If we were conditioned as children that it was not okay to say, "I'm hurt" or to object to mistreatment, then when we become adults we won't know how to respond in a healthy fashion to a husband or boss who is abusive or unduly critical of us. As women, we are especially inclined to blame ourselves instead of asking what we can do to effectively manage personal conflicts.

Good parenting prepares children to be successful in the world. Our African ancestors prepared their offspring for adulthood by putting them through rites of passage that included learning specific skills. A teenage boy who is a relative of mine participated in a specially tailored rite of passage program that included meeting with a minister to discuss his spiritual life, and with an educator to talk about his career prospects. He also met with a male nurse to discuss sex. This is what mindful parenting is all about—teaching our children specific skills from cooking to handling the challenges and prejudices they will face.

In order to be mindful parents, we must be healthy enough ourselves to pass along the emotional qualities our kids will need as adults. Once you are healthy, you will be able to share your new self with your children, who will have a better chance at becoming effective adults.

For Black American women, being an effective individual means having the abilities to:

- live in the world once your parents are gone
- establish meaningful connections with others
- greet life with the emotional skills needed for success in work and relationships

The result of such abilities is an effective woman able to develop to her fullest potential emotionally, physically, and spiritually–a woman whose dream will *not* be deferred. Such a woman is also able to meet the needs of her own children, and send them strong out into the world.

PATTERNS OF COPING, FOR BETTER AND FOR WORSE

Coping skills are the means we use to meet the challenges we face. We learn how to cope early on, from the people who are our examples, our role models—usually our parents. When we speak of "our last nerve," we mean we've almost run out of coping skills.

Some people are blessed because they have learned how to solve problems, find jobs and keep them, and, in general, improve their lives by planning for the future. Other people, however, have learned behavior that only deepens their mental distress and may lead to depression, anxiety, general ineffectiveness, substance abuse, and even violence and self-destruction.

Nobody has to be locked into childhood emotional patterns. We are free to grow up. We are free to find "mental health."

Black American women too often remain stuck in behaviors they learned as children, even if what they learned was negative. But nobody has to be locked into childhood emotional patterns. We are free to grow up. We are free to find "mental health."

THE MEANING OF "MENTAL HEALTH"

What is mental health? The following points add up to an answer.

Acceptance of Oneself

You must accept responsibility for *all* of your thoughts, feelings, and actions, which is easier said than done. Many of us have been trained to believe that certain aspects of ourselves—like aggression and sexuality—are unacceptable. If we acknowledge that these aspects are as much a part of us as the heart beating in our chests, we will accept our aggressive selves and understand that we need certain forms of aggression for both self-defense and a more action-oriented attitude toward life.

If, as children, we are bombarded with negative comments about sex, we will deny our sexual feelings as adults, and denial doesn't bode well for healthy relationships.

The Ability to Manage Life's Challenges in the Least Harmful Manner

We will all have to deal with arguments and disappointments and a variety of bad things before we shut our eyes for the last time. How do you manage? Do you turn to alcohol after a big fight with your husband? What's Plan B when there isn't enough in the checking account to pay this month's bills? *Saving Our Last Nerve* will give you positive options, such as exercise and meditation, for dealing with stress.

The Capacity to Experience Joy and Pleasure

Mentally healthy Black American women are comfortable experiencing the rewards of life. They know how to enjoy the moments when things work out. Absorb and put into practice what you learn in the following pages, and you will be able to enjoy the good moments, too.

The Ability to Tell the Difference between What is and What is not Under our Control

Many people find it tricky to tell the difference. Some of us have been raised to believe that we control *nothing*—things just happen to us. For instance, a woman might think that the lung cancer with which she was diagnosed just happened, ignoring the fact that she smoked two packs of cigarettes a day for a decade.

Some of us blame ourselves when something goes wrong in our lives or in the lives of people who are dependent upon us. We must *all* remember the Serenity Prayer:

> *God grant me*
> *the serenity to accept the things I cannot change*
> *the courage to change the things I can*
> *and the wisdom to know the difference.*

Coming to Terms with Things not under Your Control

This point, related to the last one, involves acknowledging that bad things will visit you, even though you had absolutely nothing to do with sending out the invitations. You didn't smoke, but your lungs are diseased. The tragedies of

9/11/2001 made all of us keenly aware that when we leave home disaster can strike. *Saving Our Last Nerve* will show you that even though bad things *do* happen to good people, it is not the bad that should concern you. What is important—and within your control—is how you respond.

Successful Grieving

Before we can gain strength from our disappointments, failures, and losses, we have to deal honestly with yesterday's sorrows so they can stop haunting us.

Facing the Truth

We need to make sense out of old experiences so that our new ones will be better. *Saving Our Last Nerve* will help you do that. Some readers who need more help than this book can provide may need to go into therapy and/or get on medication. Whatever course you take, being willing to seek care is a major step.

Learning to Deal with the Past

End the blame game. Your past isn't always the reason for your present predicament. Sometimes, ending that predicament requires only that you see the choices open to you now and develop the skills to shape that moment to your best advantage. And, just as importantly, dealing with the past means learning to forgive both yourself and other people.

Knowing How to Interact with Other People in Ways that are Gratifying to Both Parties

The need to have positive connections with other people is basic to your mental health.

Ongoing Self-Care

Once you have achieved at least some of your mental health objectives, you should take a more complete approach to maintaining healthfulness. That is, your mental health should work in harmony with your physical and spiritual health.

You will have to examine your good and bad habits, and you will have to discover new ways to manage stress. Eating well, exercising, and finding the faith that fulfills your needs will be part of your personal program. Maintenance may mean adding new positive fitness habits to an already tight schedule, but, as a balance, you can also get rid of the habits you don't need.

The Family Connection

When we were children, the family connection was the support system for survival. It was where we learned how to be ourselves and where we learned how to be with others. It was where our thoughts, behavior, ideals and beliefs were formed. It was our family's responsibility to nurture and shape us.... When we grow up and something goes awry in our lives, we may look back on our upbringing and find our parents guilty—guilty of being human. It seems no matter how dedicated they were in raising us, we feel we needed something more, something vital that wasn't provided.

—Susan Taylor, *In the Spirit:*
The Inspirational Writings of Susan L. Taylor[3]

Susan Taylor, editorial director of *Essence* magazine, tells us that the mental health of our families affects our education, earning potential, parenting, and relationships. If we learned a sense of hopelessness from family when we were children, we're less likely to take the actions necessary to get a good education and good jobs. We're less likely to be good parents, or to enjoy supportive and nourishing relationships.

Family is also where we learn how to deal with stress. We may witness our parents smoking a cigarette after an argument, or drinking alcohol after a tough day at work. Once we're grown and it is our turn to deal with life's challenges, we automatically turn to those early examples. If our guardians went for Kools™ and Jack Daniel's™, we're likely to go for them as well. Adults with this kind of programming are less likely to find coping strategies that work—like regular exercise, tai chi, and meditation. Such strategies will seem strange to them. Worse, such strategies may make them feel as if they're betraying those who nurtured and raised them.

I grew up in a large family and one of the ways my mother made ends meet was by shopping at consignment stores. As an adult, I continued to shop only at these stores until friends began to ask what was going on. They reminded me that I didn't have to "do the bargain-basement thing all the time." When I looked in the mirror, I saw a professional sister who could afford to shop at Lord & Taylor but didn't, because that would have seemed like abandonment and betrayal of my past. And I love my mother dearly.

We need to see that our parents made choices based on what was available to them. Sure, mother and grandmother made their macaroni and cheese dishes without worrying about cholesterol. Today, thank goodness, we know more about healthy eating than our ancestors did. We can still make macaroni and cheese, but with less harmful ingredients.

Many of our parents were poor but worked hard. Many of them weren't educated to the extent that a lot of Black women are today. Many parents were too busy just making ends meet to stop to evaluate how they were raising their children. Most parents did the best they could.

The patterns our parents instilled in many of us still control our lives. If our own parents constantly tore into us while we were growing up, we're likely to do the same to our children. If Mom, Dad, or both were stressed out and vented their rage on us, today we have to stop in the midst of our own rants to ask why we are allowing this cycle to continue. Why are we living from crisis to crisis, and spending most of our time cleaning up messes?

The Problem of Mistrust

There are some obvious, valid reasons that Black American women aren't getting the help they need to break this cycle. According to the Supplement of the Surgeon General's report on mental health, *Culture, Race and Ethnicity* many people are simply too poor and/or don't have medical insurance. [5] But the study also found another reason that we aren't getting help, one that is *within* our control: Black Americans tend not to trust the mental health establishment, and that mistrust has a history.

A lot of us didn't grow up knowing psychiatrists or psychologists or counselors, and we don't trust them because they're not familiar to us. It doesn't help that only two percent of America's psychiatrists are Black, and that law and mental health professionals have the power to lock us up. For too long, it wasn't unusual that such means were used to keep certain rebellious Black Americans in check.

But, fortunately, times have changed. Today, when mental health professionals seek involuntary evaluation or treatment, laws help guarantee that such power isn't misused.

The overriding issue is that it is unnecessary to let ourselves get to the point where we need such drastic help. Medication at the right time can save you from a serious emotional crisis. Some of my patients have told me that they are afraid that antidepressants and other related drugs will get in the way of their functioning. While it's true that the early medicines for mental illness were known occasionally to hinder functioning, today's drugs

> *Today's drugs have been proven to increase the ability to cope.*

don't have such anesthetizing side effects and have been proven to increase the ability to cope.

One patient—call her Sara—a single parent working two jobs, has relatives who are dependent on her. One, her drug-addicted brother, is high maintenance, but Sara feels an obligation to take care of him. She reluctantly hands over money when he asks for it.

When we first talked, Sara felt that taking medications would interfere with her ability to fulfill her obligations to her brother. Over several sessions, she came to see that with medication *and* therapy, she would be in a better position to put limits on her demanding sibling. For Sara, proof that my prescription worked was the day she told her brother, "You need more help than I can give. Here's the clinic number."

Women like Sara are often proud of their strength, even though they're down to their last nerve. They are living under extreme stress, but are reluctant to turn to professional counselors for help. I think they're making a mistake. Too many Black women, and Black men too, are leaving mental hurts untreated, on the ground that real men and real women don't hurt and don't need help. Often, the strongest move you can make is to admit your pain and to get the help you need.

Explaining Our Distress

Noted Harvard University psychiatrist Dr. Alvin Poussaint and co-author Amy Alexander claim in their book, *Lay My Burden Down*, that "A loss of hope and a sense of fatalism among Black Americans is key to explaining a variety of destructive and self-destructive behaviors."[4] The authors believe that racism and ongoing oppression has taken its mental and physical toll on us. Addressing our mental health needs is now mandatory if we want to be a healthy race and have strong families again.

The kind of mental health problems I often see happen because many women today have to cope with that racism and oppression and at the same time to raise families and work outside the home. As if that weren't enough, they also have to play a role in the larger family. If they fail at any of these jobs, or if they're irritable or jumpy because of the pressure, they blame themselves, and, too often, the community blames them.

These women, their families and friends, need to realize that mental distress is not always under the sufferer's control. It's as if unless we are Superwoman we consider ourselves weak or without faith. But the fact is that many of us suffer from emotional troubles. Here are some of the conditions (risk factors) that can contribute to poor mental health:

• genetic makeup
• social and cultural factors

- psychological makeup
- stress
- certain medications for birth control or high blood pressure
- thyroid problems

The Surgeon General's report lists additional social and cultural risk factors:

- severe marital difficulties
- overcrowding
- criminal behavior by the father
- mental illness in the mother
- admission to foster care

If you're having mental health problems, you're not alone.

We must stop believing that we don't suffer from the same illnesses as the larger culture. Statistics help show that the problem is widespread, and that if you're having mental health problems, you're not alone.

The Surgeon General's report on mental health discovered that twenty percent of Americans have a mental disorder over the course of any given year. Fifteen percent of them also have substance abuse problems to go along with their mental distress. About ten percent of Americans over the year will use mental health services and five percent will seek assistance from schools, religious sources, social services, or regularly help themselves exercising and/or meditating.

So, again, if you are having mental health problems, you are not alone. Sure, it's tough to confess your need, even to yourself. But to do so is an act of strength and courage, not weakness. You need to be determined to stop old habits that have driven you to the brink. And determination will help lead you to a healthier life.

You may not have a mental illness, but you probably know a friend or family member who does. Often, you can tell when your friends aren't functioning well. The clue is that they are making obvious attempts at self-medication: seeing too many men, drinking too much alcohol and/or taking drugs, eating too much food, spending too much time at the mall. Self-medications don't work, and can become a dangerous addiction.

Many of us have forgotten how to imagine that our lives can be satisfying, that we can experience tranquility. Too often we hang on to the belief that we were destined for hard lives. We accept our burdens because we saw others accepting theirs. Why would our plight be any different? But it *can* be different. You just need to walk the necessary steps on the path to good mental health. You just need to be determined

> *Self-medications don't work, and can become a dangerous addiction.*

Brenda Moves On....

Our work together helped Brenda identify her symptoms of depression and realize she had suffered from the disorder on and off at least since her teen years. She was able to see how her depression had driven her to drop out of college because she was unable to retain information. She also came to the conclusion that her mother and several aunts had most likely suffered from depression.

At first she was hesitant to try medication because she felt she was being used as an experiment, but she finally agreed to give it a try. The medication helped control her symptoms and improved her work performance enough to allow her to keep her job. Her boss and her friends marveled at the miraculous change. But to herself, Brenda says, "Miracle, my eye." She knows that it's been a miracle of hard work, work that paid off.

Steps to Optimum Mental Health

- Take some time to review your family history and the strengths it provided you.
- Remember to give yourself credit for being interested in your mental health and reading this book.
- List any beliefs or fears you have about mental illness and consider how they might get in the way of your seeking help.
- Ask other people how they view mental health and if they would they consider seeking help if they needed it.

MORE FOR YOUR HEALTH
Book

Maya Angelou: *I Know Why the Caged Bird Sings.* New York: Bantam Books. 1970

Movies

A Raisin in the Sun, The Color Purple, Straight Out of Brooklyn. These movies reveal how family dynamics impact family members.

Chapter Two

The Sheep are as Good as the Pasture in Which They Graze

The Myth of the Strong Black Female

Aggressive Adolescents who Act Out Their Own Version of the Myth

Stephanie

Whenever Stephanie walked into the women's section at the local department store, the salesclerks whispered to each other, "Ka-ching. Ka-ching." Their commissions were bound to spike that day because Stephanie was a spendthrift *par excellence*. Her shopping addiction was so overwhelming that she left the tags on most of the goods she bought so she could exchange them for more stuff when the cash and credit cards were tapped out.

In my office, Stephanie described the excitement and pleasure she would experience during these shopping trips. Unfortunately, such feelings were short-lived. Shopping gave her only a brief interlude from her feelings of powerlessness and despair.

By the time Stephanie came in for her first appointment

with me, she'd already done some of the work. She was vaguely aware that she shopped more when she was angry with her husband or her boss. But she felt powerless to change the pattern. She'd decided it was "genetic," since her mother and sisters all did the same thing. So my work was cut out for me. It was my job to convince Stephanie that she *had* control where she thought she had none.

The Old Dance of Emotions and Thoughts

Remember "the hustle" or "slow drag?" Sometimes, when you are alone, you might still find yourself dancing as you did so many times at your favorite disco or house party. You became so familiar with the steps to the dance and the accompanying body movements that your body was in a call and response pattern of give and take.

Imagine your emotions and thoughts being a dance between two partners. Just as hearing the music brings the old dance moves back, so certain situations prompt the same old emotional response.

Your emotional patterns were established early, before you had any control over them. A child can't choose the experiences she's shaped by. And now those same feelings you learned as a child shape your experiences as an adult. It's as if you have to keep reliving some lost moment in childhood. You seek out partners who dance in the same way you did before. After all, who wants to learn new steps when the old ones are so familiar? It's like that cartoon from *Ebony* magazine, where an older woman complains to a younger one that her new husband is the same as her first, second and third. It's as if by repeating the same old game we'll eventually learn and get it right.

But the fact is that we can't get it right till we learn to play a different game that has different rules. Until we can do that, we go on humming our tune: *this time if I sacrifice my needs enough, they will truly understand, appreciate me, and finally give me what I want.*

Difficulties arise when, as adults, we continue to use old or outdated methods of interacting with others that have limited effectiveness. Standing in front of others in our Easter outfit was cute when we were four, but it looks quite different at forty. It takes work to identify the pattern we are repeating and to discover what thoughts or wishes are the driving forces behind the behavior.

During our youth we must develop a measure of success balancing our inner drives against the demands imposed upon us from outside. We must make some degree of peace with the part of us that seeks connection to others and the part that feels aggression and hostility toward others. It is a delicate balance, and depending upon the choices we make, it will determine how much inner peace or turmoil we experience.

Good Nurture as Prevention

Have you ever cared for houseplants or worked in a garden? Such a pastime teaches us that the health of a plant depends on how much light and water it gets and the quality of the soil—that is, depends on nurture outside the plant itself.

Envision a young Black American girl planted in the household of her upbringing. What nutrients, light, and care does *she* require to be able to eventually pack her bags and move out into the world to make a new world of her own and thrive?

Too often she doesn't get the required sustenance and nurture when she's a child. When that happens, she may grow up to be a wounded adult who requires years of psychological counseling in order to realize her full potential strength.

The Soil We Grow In

The path of self-discovery begins with a clear understanding of the soil in which we grew up. That means asking yourself the questions and patiently reflecting for answers: "What sort of soil did I grow up in? What strengths did it give me? What deficiencies in it left me searching for more fertile soil?"

In our families we are given rules to live by, but we generally learn more by the examples we see. Few of us are surprised when we hear that a boy who watched his mother being beaten by her lover grows into a man who beats his girlfriend. What the boy witnessed didn't in itself guarantee that he would be abusive. It just meant that the abusive man who beat his mother became a negative role model for the child. Had the boy been luckier, he might have had other, more positive male role models. As it is, he's learned a destructive behavior. Only with the help of psychological counseling can he *unlearn* it.

You too are probably aware of harmful patterns learned in childhood. You tell yourself you won't repeat them. But without help it is hard to free yourself from destructive, often self-destructive, behaviors.

Some Basic Terms

For your journey, you'll need a few tools. Looking at oneself is complicated by the fact that, often, without being aware, we filter our experience through particular lenses, and we find ways to soften truths that might be too painful to experience directly. Psychologists have given names to the ways we process our experience. By learning these basic concepts, you'll be better prepared for your journey and better able to understand and talk to your doctor or psychologist. So keep these key terms in mind.

Repression involves keeping out of our consciousness thoughts, feelings, and desires that are unacceptable to us. An example might be the inability to recall the name of a teacher who was particularly hurtful. Keeping this name from your awareness helps limit the anger you want to control.

Suppression involves the conscious decision to put unacceptable thoughts, emotions, and ideas out of our awareness. " I am not going to think about how rude that salesclerk was to me anymore." Instead, you choose to think and feel other emotions and thoughts.

Denial involves the quality of disbelief. For example, you saw your boyfriend give his phone number to an attractive woman, but you convince yourself you didn't see it. You do this so you won't have to experience thoughts and feelings that will cause you anxiety or rage.

Displacement speaks to our tendency to move our "unacceptable" feelings from one person to another. You may be extremely angry at your grandmother but feel too anxious to confront her and so you get into an argument with your sister. Or you may be angry at a husband or boss, and get into an argument with a stranger—or even a friend.

Projection involves putting, or transferring, onto others our own unacceptable thoughts, feelings, or impulses. The minister is attracted to you, as opposed to you being attracted to him. Or, "That person wants to do me harm and I'd better protect myself." Projection occurs outside of your awareness and decreases any anxiety you would feel about your desire to connect with the minister, or, in the second case, about your own aggression.

Rationalization involves offering a reasonable explanation for why certain unreasonable and "unacceptable" thoughts, desires, behaviors occurred. You explain that you drove three miles out of your way because you wanted to avoid a possible traffic jam, but in fact you did so to avoid the anxiety you would feel driving across the bridge.

Dissociation involves separating parts of our mental activity or actions from our conscious functioning. You discover several items in your closet you don't remember buying, although no one else could have placed them there.

Identification entails taking on behaviors or ideas from another individual and making them your own. After the death of your favorite aunt, for instance, you begin to dress in purple because it was her favorite color. We can also learn tastes and prejudices in this way.

Identification with the Aggressor happens when we take on behaviors, thoughts, or feelings that belong to another, usually harmful person. The rejection of Black Americans by

Black Americans is an important example. We are identifying with the majority culture that sometimes feels and exhibits hostility toward Black Americans.

Intellectualization is using logic or intellectual means to avoid dealing with our discomfort about certain feelings or desires. An example would be the student who tells herself that the pursuit of academic achievement is much more important than going out on dates because of fears about intimacy.

Isolation happens when feelings are separated from their associated thoughts. You are able to speak nonchalantly, without anxiety or anger, about the murder of a neighbor.

Reaction Formation involves feeling and/or behaving in a manner that is the opposite of an unacceptable feeling or impulse. You are furious at your brother, but instead of letting yourself be aware of it, you invite him and his girlfriend to a home-cooked meal.

Sublimation is the means by which unacceptable drives or desires are directed toward norms that society sees as acceptable. You are sexually aroused by your girlfriend's husband and go run four miles on your treadmill.

In *Undoing* we attempt to take back something we have deemed unacceptable that makes us feel anxious. After making a harmful comment about your friend, you talk about how wonderful she really is.

Regression is a means of returning to a previous manner of relating. After being successfully toilet-trained, a four-year-old begins to wet herself when the new baby has her diaper changed.

Substitution is where we exchange wishes or feelings that seem unacceptable for wishes or feelings we feel less anxious about. You want to angrily attack your boss, but allow yourself to only feel mild irritation against him.

PATTERNS OF COPING,
FOR BETTER AND FOR WORSE

The terms above all point to the ways we manage internal feelings, thoughts, and external stress. They can be thought of as "coping strategies." We may use one coping strategy or several at a time and most of us find certain ones that seem to work best. Unfortunately, we often keep using coping strategies in spite of the fact that they repeatedly leave us frustrated because our needs are not really being met.

Let's take a common example. Say you were raised in a family where your mother was overworked and had little time or energy left to nurture you or your brothers and sisters. You may have learned to deny your feelings of dependency and your need for help and reassurance. You might even deny these feelings with a strong sense of independence, saying, " I don't need anyone."

Many of us have felt that way all our lives and managed to be reasonably successful in school and work. But in our relationships with other people, we don't find satisfaction. We have this nagging sense that, for all our trying, no one really cares for us. Yet still we feel "comfortable" doing for ourselves and everyone else and never allowing others to do anything for us.

This means that behind a lot of women who, to themselves and others, appear to be superwomen, is the little girl who needed more than what her mother was able to provide. It also means that we'd rather go on doing things that hurt us than change. Yes, change can be as difficult as that.

I've used the example of the woman who takes all the responsibility for herself and others and gets nothing in return. But we see a similar kind of behavior among adolescent girls. Increasingly, we encounter angry teens on the street or mall or subway train. They have their " kick em to the curb" attitude written all over themselves.

These girls have often seen several generations of strong Black women to draw upon for justification of their protective front. But while those generations of women have learned that strength, they have also had to deal with being abandoned by mates and with the difficulties and dangers that a woman, who may also be a mother, must face when she's alone.

For the girls, as for the mothers and grandmothers, it isn't "cool" to reveal their deep feelings of sadness, grief, and rage, so they substitute feelings (sometimes aggressive) that are more acceptable to those around them and to themselves.

Many of these young women have not dealt with feelings of grief and loss surrounding absent fathers or fathers who were physically present but unavailable emotionally. In therapy, it is possible to learn how these unmet needs can lead Black American women to have unrealistic expectations of male partners. We can face, with help, our desire to have a father substitute in our relationships. We will also be able to deal with anger that is sometimes directed toward our mothers, perhaps blaming her for driving the father off. Even more importantly, we will be able to deal with the self-directed anger we have developed because we blame ourselves for driving the father away with our neediness or feeling that we aren't acceptable.

Getting past this super cool front takes work, patience, and courage to tolerate the unpleasant feelings many women try so desperately to avoid. Such feelings come from unmet needs, unresolved losses, grief, and chronic anxiety. They show themselves in the unhealthy behaviors in which we participate.

> *Getting past this super cool front takes work, patience, and courage.*

When we trap these feelings inside they come back to torment us and affect our behavior. Such buried feeling can become too painful to tolerate.

That's when we may start to "externalize"—because we feel bad and look for something outside of ourselves to make us feel better or acceptable. One common way of making ourselves feel better is to shop for status products or for products that can alter our appearance or the way we present ourselves to the world. Black Americans are major consumers of cosmetics, hair products, status cars (BMWs, Mercedes Benz), and more. Buying such things may be an attempt to soothe the pain. The only trouble is, it doesn't work.

In *Women Who Shop Too Much,* Carolyn Wesson writes about women addicted to shopping: "They have found a way to feel better about themselves, and, at the same time, they have discovered a sure-fire way to banish unwanted thoughts, feelings, and problems. Some of the feelings they want to escape from are emptiness, depression, anxiety, anger, powerlessness and rejection."[5]

Shopping as self-therapy is common enough in American culture in general. Our passion for materialism is obvious to us and to Madison Avenue as well. But what's especially clear is the Black American woman's passion for altering her external appearance with endless shopping sprees. The source of such sprees may be the feeling some of us have all of the time and all of us have some of the time: we are not good enough, or attractive enough, to succeed. Stephanie would learn, after several months of working with me, that feelings like this were behind her shopping sprees. But too many Black women still have that lesson to learn.

SUICIDE ON THE INSTALLMENT PLAN
Sharon

We learn by example how to survive in a world that hurts us regularly with ongoing racism, sexism, and "classism." Often, mere survival leaves us weary of the struggle and wanting to numb ourselves rather than experience harsh realities. So we keep adding layers of insulation to the unpleasant feelings within us, and continue in denial.

Black women are often said to be committing suicide on the installment plan. That means we engage in behaviors that don't kill us directly but in the long run shorten our lives.

Let's look at Sharon, for example. On weekends she likes to drink, sometimes, she admits, a little too much. Recently at a party, after she'd had several wine coolers, she met a man she fell for, even though she didn't know much more about him than that he dressed fine and drove a Mercedes SUV.

They had sex without a condom because he assured her he was very selective about his sexual partners. After all, wasn't he sleeping with her? But later, after she'd almost forgotten him, she developed vaginal warts. She went in for examination and treatment of the condition, but found the examination embarrassing, and, after the first year, neglected her yearly Pap smear. Two years later, Sharon was diagnosed with cervical cancer that had spread to her bones.

Sharon never took an overdose or shot herself, but the cause of death on her death certificate should read "suicide." And you *know* it didn't have to be that way.

CAN WE BE *TOO* FAITHFUL TO OUR FAMILY AND OUR PAST?

One of the difficulties with changing our behavior sometimes has to do with a blind loyalty to our past, which may also be loyalty to one's family. For example,

- My grandmother and mother always made fried corn. They used close to a pound of butter and heavy cream. How could I not do the same?
- My mother and grandma did all the things they had to do without ever complaining or showing anger. What right do I have to act differently?

We feel that if we change, if we break the pattern, we are in some way cutting our ancestral ties. That's why we feel guilty when we make choices that don't include our families, and that sometimes carry us away from them and their values.

Letting ourselves become aware of how much we want to keep our families around allows us to consciously make choices that are good for us. We still love and respect them, but we have to separate ourselves in order to flourish. We can remember the African proverb, "Try this bracelet, if it fits, wear it, but if it hurts you, throw it away no matter how shiny." The ways of those we love are like the shiny bracelet: we don't want to give them up, but must we sacrifice ourselves for a sense of connection?

Our resistance to seeking mental health care sometimes comes from a sense of loyalty to the family members who have gone before us. Our mothers, aunts, and grandmothers struggled and sacrificed. They never ate at fancy restaurants or had someone help keep the house. How could we possibly pay someone to help us handle our stress better when they never did? Do we think we are better than they were? Or are we not as strong?

Our resistance to seeking mental health care sometimes comes from a sense of loyalty to the family members who have gone before us.

Another reason we may resist help is that we may not feel worthy of receiving it. Feeling worthy is something we learn or don't learn from the people who care for us when we're children. Our caregivers serve as mirrors in which we see ourselves. If they don't know how to give us a sense of self worth, probably because they don't feel worthy themselves, we will feel that others are more acceptable, more deserving, and better than we are. We don't know how to give ourselves an okay signal because we don't have confidence that we can change or that we are worth the effort.

For many of us, this hesitancy and confusion are part of the legacy of racism. The renowned Algerian psychiatrist Frantz Fanon wrote about this legacy decades ago in *Black Skins, White Masks.*[6] He said it was impossible to live in a racist culture without taking in some of the racist beliefs ourselves. That is, living in a culture of people who so often appear to despise us, we begin to hate ourselves.

During slavery, we lost some capacity to love ourselves and to love others. Now it is time to heal ourselves. In this new century, unless we are willing to look at our own pain and rejection, we will continue to produce young people who are unable to look into our eyes and feel loved, acceptable, and worthy.

HOW TO FIND HELP

First, to determine whether your difficulties might be related to a health problem like diabetes or thyroid illness, schedule an appointment with your primary care doctor. Be sure to follow the recommendations for a Pap smear and a mammogram. Once we hit "the big forty," we should have these tests done yearly unless our doctor recommends otherwise.

Let your doctor know about your mental health concerns. Many doctors have screening tools available or can give you the name of a mental health provider to whom they can refer you. If your doctor can not provide you with a resource, ask your spiritual leader, or call the National Mental Health Association, 1–800–969–NMHA. The NMHA can direct you to mental health resources in your area.

If you are thinking of harming yourself, you can call 1–800–SUICIDE, or go to your nearest emergency room.

If you do not have health insurance, your state department of health should have a mental health component that can give you information about clinics or individuals who will see you at a fee based on your income, or for no fee at all..

Stephanie Moves On....

Over time, Stephanie was able to identify her coping style of acting out her feelings instead of putting them into words. Her shopping sprees were her way of acting out her fear that her husband would get angry and leave her if she expressed her own anger and disappointment with him.

Breaking this pattern was easier said than done, particularly since she received so much support for her shopping behavior from others. It was necessary for Stephanie to develop an anger management plan that included keeping a journal, exercise, and taking assertiveness training. She also was able to decrease her buying by using a forty-eight hour rule. She could identify items she would like to buy but she had to think about the purchase for two days before she could buy nonessential items.

> *Stephanie was able to decrease her buying by using a forty-eight hour rule.*

This strategy allowed her enough time to explore the feelings that fueled her shopping urge.

STEPS TO OPTIMUM MENTAL HEALTH

Take some time to consider the coping patterns you have developed that might not be working as effectively as you would like. Do you find, for instance, that you are avoiding certain jobs because they would require you to be more assertive? Do all your relationships (even the good ones) end in the same fashion? Consider whether you are experiencing enough discontent in your life to take additional steps toward achieving more pleasure.

MORE FOR YOUR HEALTH
Book

Barras, Jonetta Rose: *Whatever Happened to Daddy's Little Girl? The Impact of Fatherlessness on Black Women.* New York: The Ballantine Publishing Group, 2000

Movie

Men of Honor. The main character and his wife demonstrate how childhood experiences shaped their current choices.

CHAPTER THREE

ONE DOES NOT CROSS THE RIVER WITHOUT GETTING WET

How to Recognize and Cope with Stress Common to the Black American Woman

Darlene

As she stood before the mirror getting dressed, Darlene noticed that the waistband of her favorite black dress was frayed. And when she looked at her face, she saw what she knew already—her nerves were more worn than the dress. She sighed, and headed out the door on her way to another funeral, as she'd done too many times in recent years.

Too many of her friends were dying from AIDS, but nobody seemed to get the message. Even her best friend, Michelle, would say, when Darlene tried to reason with her: "You have to die from something." Those words echoed in Darlene's head as she waited for the bus, on her way to the funeral of another AIDS victim, her cousin Alan. Just two months earlier, she'd gone to the funeral of Alan's partner.

Darlene's sadness had become consuming, and when she

tried to talk to friends they didn't have time. "Nobody has to die of AIDS," she'd tell them. But no one wanted to listen. She attended grief support group sessions, but they didn't help. The deaths had left her feeling abandoned, frightened, and defenseless.

LEARNING TO GRIEVE

Along the path of life, losses, failures, and disappointments often come our way. The Buddha said there are ten thousand joys and ten thousand sorrows. But many of us are shocked when things don't go as planned or expected. We live somehow believing we will escape what every human being must experience.

A Zen story tells us of a woman who has lost her child to illness. She approaches a Zen Master, and asks that the burden of this tragedy be lifted from her shoulders. Yes, he says, but first she must go to every household in the village and find one that has not been struck by tragedy. Needless to say, she is unable to find one. And this was his lesson: tragedy comes to us all and we must learn the best ways to deal with it.

Learning this truth, to put it mildly, isn't easy. Sometimes we make matters worse by blaming ourselves when no blame is appropriate. Sometimes we make matters worse by thinking how we did everything right but still we were made to suffer. Either way, we feed the sense of loss with the conviction that this suffering is unique to us.

We all want to believe that because we have acted the right way we will be spared life's pains, but, of course, none of us is spared. At the very least, we all grow old, and sick, and die. And sometimes, like Darlene, we have to suffer things that we don't individually have the power to change.

The tragic events of 9/11/2001 simply showed us once again what life tries to teach us all along: disaster can just come out of the sky, in the blink of an eye, and destroy innocent lives.

Too often, even as we tell other people and ourselves that we have accepted some loss, deep down we still try to undo it, still try to reverse the past so the event never happens, so our lives can return to what they were before and we can feel safer. Yet people who believe they are in control may find themselves especially unprepared when challenges or disasters land on their doorsteps, and often hide their pain and grief very well.

Losing successfully is a hard game, and few people have been taught to play it well. We pity ourselves and seek pity from others. Self-pity and sympathy from other people may provide a certain temporary comfort, but they don't take care of business. Ultimately, taking care of the business of grieving means getting on with our lives. But to do that, first we must truly have grieved. Successful grieving is a kind of healing. Yes, it leaves scars, but it allows us to continue to function, sometimes stronger than before, because we have faced our grief honestly in the depth of our hearts.

> *Successful grieving is a kind of healing.*

Self-pity can stand in the way of "successful grieving," and we need to look at its sources. We get caught in self-pity because we walk around with daydreams of how things should be. Our dreams may be made up of the following elements:

- an ideal family, one in which we are loved and affirmed.
- a financially stable existence

- a comfortable home
- the ideal that the people we love—spouses, parents, grandparents, children, friends—will remain in our lives forever
- that we will be young and healthy forever
- that we will live in a society that loves and affirms us
- that we will be loved unconditionally
- that we will have a spouse who will love us forever

When any of these dream-expectations break down, we may feel that we've somehow been betrayed.

An Exercise

Take some time now to go through the "dream" list on page 41–42. What are your own dreams in each case, and how do those dreams match with reality? After you've thought about it for a while, write them down in two columns—the dream and the reality. (Use a journal for these exercises—the kind of composition book you can pick up in any drug store will do the trick.) You may find that the results mean giving up certain expectations about life, which is, in itself, of great value. The exercise can help you to see things not as they "should be" but as they are. Then you may be free to grieve.

SUCCESSFUL GRIEVING

Successful grieving means coming to healthy terms with loss. It means accepting that someone or something we were deeply attached to is gone and can't be brought back. Even the changes that come with time can be reason for grief. Losing your teeth, or suffering some other sign that your body is breaking down—that can be a cause of grief. So can a change in other people, even something as simple as a good friend you always shared smoking breaks with in the freezing weather deciding to kick the habit. Instead of taking inspiration from the friend's good sense to quit smoking, you might grieve the loss of that companionship.

Remember the fable, *The Wonderful Tar Baby Story*, about the Fox's schemes to capture Br'er Rabbit? In one such scheme he places a "baby" covered with tar in the middle of the road. When Br'er Rabbit happens upon Tar Baby, he tries to start a conversation. When the Tar Baby remains silent, Br'er rabbit grows furious. Finally, he hits Tar Baby and his paw becomes stuck. He strikes Tar Baby with the other paw, and it too becomes stuck. Soon, he has hit Tar Baby with most of his body and is helplessly caught.

In a way, our attachment to others is similar to Br'er Rabbit's. When people don't respond to us as we think they should, we lash out. And something similar can happen when a loved one dies. Though they are gone—*because* they are gone—our attachment remains strong, and sometimes we may need professional help in the agonizing process of becoming unattached.

When some of us were children, our parents taught us that losses are replaceable. We might have lost a pet bird and right away received another one before we acknowledged and grieved the loss. For others of us, when someone dear to us died, we were given no guidance by adults as to how to cope with our grief and profound sense of loss. We all know women who never seem to get it right, and whose first response to losing a partner is immediately to jump in bed with another man.

Coping with loss means taking time. Yes, you're after a kind of closure, but you're willing to let it come slowly. You know that you must bear the pain and not hurry it. Other people will urge you to forget a grief before you are ready to do so. But only you can decide how long the grieving process must take. Given enough time and work, your emotions will heal, and you will be able to give your love new channels. Slowly, you will find an appetite for life again. Gradually, you will be open to other people again, able to enjoy what you used to enjoy, and maybe some new things too. Life does go on. But only when we allow ourselves to feel our grief fully.

> *Coping with loss means taking time.*

What can make the grieving process especially difficult is when we have some "unfinished business" with the person whom we've lost: *If only my mother had been able to appreciate my dark skin; if only my father could apologize for not seeing me as an individual.* Or: *If only I'd loved more generously, if only I'd given what the other person asked of me.*

We become fixed on such unfinished business. We may also become fixed on strong needs and desires we experienced as children if these needs weren't met. For example, you were an aspiring dancer as a girl and your mother missed all your major performances. You wanted her love and affirmation but you never received it. Now that you are grown, you may still be seeking it—if not from your mother, from other people. You find yourself playing out the childhood scene over and over, and each time you end up feeling rejected. You keeping chang-ing your dance partners, but you are still trying to dance the same two-step or hustle you learned so long ago.

In *The Grief Recovery Handbook: A Step-by-Step Program for Moving Beyond Loss*, authors John W. James and Frank Cherry note that we want the lost relationship in some way to have been different, better, or more.[7] But wallowing in "what-if" thinking doesn't allow us to move forward to new relation-ships. Yes, the truth of loss can be painful, but it's the begin-ning of healing.

Unfortunately, our culture has taught us myths that hin-der our ability to do the work of grieving. At a funeral service, we may try to comfort a bereaved friend, but then, in the more difficult period that follows, we leave the person alone with grief. It's as if we truly believe that grief is something we could leave behind at the graveside. Fortunately, today some funeral homes and churches provide support programs that can help see mourners through the entire grieving process. If your church doesn't have such a program, talk to the Mental Health Association. They can refer you to a grief support group in your area or can help your church organize a group of its own. (For more information on organizing your church into a health-aware community, see *Congregational Health: How to Make Your Church a Health-Aware Community*.)[8]

Perhaps because other people are impatient with our grief, we become afraid to acknowledge how much we are hurting. Again and again in my own practice I see patients who are "fronting." It takes all my effort and ingenuity to break through the front, which is often that of the strong Black woman. These women are hemorrhaging inside, unable to do the work of grieving. "They who conceal their disease cannot expect to be cured," goes an African proverb.

An Exercise

In a journal, set aside about ten pages to work on loss and disappointments over the next several weeks. Beginning with your early childhood, list the major losses and hurts you have experienced. *The Grief Recovery Handbook* recommends you list the losses in the order in which they happened, so you can learn how losses can build upon each other.[9] Next to each item, note and explore how you coped with the losses. Here's an example of what such a list might look like:

· *Age three, my younger sister was born. This was difficult for me because now my folks were very busy with her and I didn't get much attention.*
· *Age five, my dog died after being hit by a car. I felt guilty that I had let him run without his leash.*
· *Age seven, I begged my parents for a bicycle like my girlfriend's. I was given some used skates.*
· *Age ten, I broke my arm while wrestling with my brother's friends. My parents were angry with me for being a tomboy. I really wanted their comfort, but was scolded instead.*

LEARNING TO RE-PARENT YOURSELF

As you identify the losses and your responses, you will start seeing how old losses may still contribute to the discontent you are currently experiencing. While you can't go back and change what happened, you can, as an adult, learn to let go of some of those unfulfilled wishes.

For many people, spirituality provides the path for finding meaning in the disappointments and losses they have experienced. Lessons and blessings can be found in loss. We need to move past the self-pitying phase and search for the growth potential; sometimes, you only need to shift your perspective. In *Finding God*, Dr. Kevin W. Cosby challenges the reader not to look for God to lighten the load off her back, but to strengthen her back to carry the load: "Do not pray for an easy life, pray to become a stronger person. Do not pray for tasks equal to your powers, but pray for powers equal to your tasks."[9]

> *Lessons and blessings can be found in loss.*

Some of us grew up neglected and even abused. For us to heal we have to commit to *re-parenting* ourselves. That doesn't mean looking for new substitutes for the failed relationships of the past. It doesn't mean jumping from relationship to relationship, or trying to ease our wounds with drug, alcohol, sex, food, or, for that matter, desperate shopping. It means finding the powers we need for true self-renewal.

The essence of healing is to become one's own good parent. First, you must suffer the loss of having imperfect parents. Then *you* can learn to give yourself the feeling of worthiness you crave, to give yourself the respect you need, and

> *The essence of healing is to become one's own good parent.*

to make yourself worthy of healthy love. What you didn't get as a child, you can have as an adult, *by learning to appreciate and celebrate your own specialness*. To reach this point, you first have to accept the loss of having imperfect parents, or at least parents who in some ways, weren't a good match for you.

For those of us who didn't have strong and affirming relationships while growing up, the healing process starts by recognizing this emotional wound. Linda Hollies, in her book, *Inner Healing for Broken Vessels: Seven Steps to a Woman's Way of Healing*, writes that healing the hurt child is possible when you

- admit that the wound has power over you
- experience the pain
- share the wound (break the silence)
- accept the past
- choose to have a present that is different[10]

Jonetta Rose Barras sums up these points eloquently in *Whatever Happened to Daddy's Little Girl? The Impact of Fatherlessness on Black Women:* "We can never become mature adult women until we honor that little girl in us," she writes, "telling her, in language she understands, that she is without blame for the course her life took."[11] With support throughout the process, women can successfully grieve over the loss they feel of not having been lovingly fathered. At the same time, they can discover the strength they developed because of the necessity of parenting themselves.

You remember the poem:

Humpty Dumpty sat on a wall; Humpty Dumpty had a great fall.

All the King's horses and all the King's men,
Couldn't put Humpty Dumpty back together again.

What too many of us learned from this story was that if you fall, it is all over. So we tried to avoid falling at all costs. The lesson we must learn now is that we can fall and get up, bruised knees, or hearts, and all. And that's the lesson we must also teach our children—they may fall, and they may get up again. Yes, we and our children can learn to get up, not with the help of all the King's horses and all the King's men, but by our own choice, our own effort. The old folks would call it pulling yourself up by your own bootstraps.

Achieving mental health requires a game plan. Here are some reminders as you prepare for the task:

- be patient. As Gladys Knight sang in *Overnight Success,* it doesn't happen overnight.
- expect disappointments and learn how to handle them.

You need to be a good coach, not a heckling fan in the crowd.

The key, as we struggle upward, is how to handle setbacks. Sure, figure out where and how your mistakes may have contributed to setbacks, but don't stay locked in the notion that bad things happen because there's something inherently wrong with you. You need to be a good coach, not a heckling fan in the crowd.

RAISING STRONG CHILDREN

While adults can be cured of bad emotional habits, the best thing is to raise children who won't be handicapped, because

An Exercise

Think about a recent disappointment you have experienced—one in which you were required to perform. For example, you were asked to make a presentation and it bombed. What did you say to yourself afterwards?

· They were out to get me anyway. _____

· I am always messing up. _____

· Why do I even try? _____

· I didn't do as well as I would have liked. _____

The thoughts you choose after a disappointment shape your feelings. Yes, you can make a choice by shifting your focus from that loud buzz word *failure* to a different focal point, a different, positive buzzword. Evaluate yourself, noting two or three things you did to your satisfaction. Then you can take up one or two items that you will work on to improve your next presentation or another performance. Be patient with yourself. Performance of almost any kind depends on the old formula: practice, practice, practice.

they have learned how to fail successfully. If they fall off a bike or off the monkey bars, help them build the skills they will need for the larger falls they will certainly encounter on life's journey. Otherwise, they will go through life afraid of falling and avoiding all experiences in which they might fail. That's how people sentence themselves to lives of limited possibilities. Instead of using natural aggression to overcome obstacles, they identify themselves as the obstacle to be overcome, endlessly caught in self-blame, and endlessly holding back from the challenge that could help them grow.

Bad Homes, Good People

Children are harmed by not getting the encouragement and affirmation they need. True, many of us recover from that harm and grow up to be reasonably effective adults. But to do so, we have had to struggle against those early conditions.

Remember, I'm talking about homes where the following conditions were the norm:

- abuse (emotional, physical, and sexual)
- alcohol or substance abuse
- episodes of rage

In *On Playing a Poor Hand Well,* Mark Katz, notes that the people who best prevail over difficult childhoods can talk about their early traumatic experiences.[12] Talking about them opens up new ways of seeing them. You can learn to see that the person who is really responsible for the experience is not yourself, but your drunken father or angry mother—the adult who taught you to be afraid, to hide, and to expect failure.

I do not wish to suggest that children who grow up in highly stressful households always need therapy when they become adults. Many of us have learned to draw on other resources that compensate for what our parents failed to give us. According to researchers Emmy E. Werner and Ruth S. Smith, authors of *Overcoming the Odds: High Risk Children from Birth to Adulthood*, these resources can come from several places:

- natural attributes of the child: for example, a child is artistically inclined and turns to painting early, learning confidence and freedom of expression
- other family members who offer protection from abusive parents or guardians: an aunt or uncle offers the child comfort when the child's own parent goes off on an emotional rampage
- community members become protectors: an English teacher, for example, who is willing to listen to the child and offer affirmation.[13]

Black American women who can't find, or don't have, these resources available may come out of childhood fearing success. We believe that bad things happened to us as children because we were bad girls. Such negative thinking stifles initiative—we won't even try. Sometimes we anticipate fearfully that if we are successful we may have to stand alone. We may find it easier to be unsuccessful than to deal with rejection, because, when we were kids, no one was in our corner to tell us that rejection is part of life.

Rejection in the form of criticism sometimes comes from the people closest to us. As I pushed on with my studies and career, I heard plenty of criticism from friends and family members who didn't want to be left behind: "Oh, she thinks she's better than us," or, "Oh, now she's got so smart she is going to move out of the neighborhood." But even without destructive criticism, we may generate our own accusing thoughts and fear that our success could isolate us from the people we love. It doesn't have to be that way. *Black American women* can *succeed and still keep strong ties with their community.*

LIVING WITH CHANGE

Our "identity," who we are, isn't set in stone, as we might imagine. It changes constantly as each day brings new experiences and challenges. We must always be ready to grow, and that isn't always easy. Even though life *is* about change, we are resistant to change, especially in relation to loss, disappointment, or pain. We find it hard to let go of the comfortable old self. We find it hard to give up a relationship even when the relationship is obviously over. We don't want to give up our old ways of coping or the often fruitless dreams we invented to take the bite out of our suffering. Before we can change, we must find meaning in our suffering. Only then can we let it go and learn to live with old wounds and, slowly, to let them heal.

In his introduction to Victor Frankl's *Man's Search for Meaning*, Gordon Allport writes: "To live is to suffer, to survive is to find meaning in the suffering."[14] Frankl, a psychiatrist who survived the Nazi concentration camps, gained that knowledge from a terrible experience. The saving truth he harvested from the camps was that: "Everything can be taken from a man but one thing: the last of the human freedoms, to choose one's attitude in any given circumstance is to choose one's own way."

In one of his sermons, Dr. Kevin Cosby, pastor of St. Stephen Baptist Church in Louisville, Kentucky, told this story about a farmer who had a small farm, a wife, a son, and a horse. One day his horse ran away and his neighbors said, "It's a bad day." The farmer said, "I can't agree because all my days aren't in yet." The following day, the horse returned with several wild horses. The neighbors, noting all the animals, now said, "Guess it's a good day." The farmer replied, "I can't really say, all my days aren't in yet." The following day, his only son

An Exercise

An important part of the healing process is to identify the dreams or hopes you associate with your losses—that is, the experiences and even long episodes of your life that you look back at with regret and pain. You can learn to identify dreams and hopes in any of several ways using:

· your own everyday awareness
· self-examination
· books like this one
· support groups with other people who have had similar experiences
· therapy

Although it can be painful to finally acknowledge the real loss: the father who wasn't there, the lover who proved false, or some ideal notion you had of yourself but somehow betrayed, this acknowledgment can put you in touch with strength you never had.

Remember, what you are looking for is not the surface of the event but the deeper meaning. You may find, for example, when you look into a former relationship, that it wasn't love you were getting or even looking for, but being admired by others because you'd been chosen by a particular partner. Or maybe you were simply tired of being lonely. Or you hoped the relationship would give you a better social life. Of course, only you can find the true meaning of a lost hope or dream.

continued on next page

---

continued from previous page

To start exploring:

Identify the dreams associated with each of your major losses and disappointments: An example might be the relationship you thought would last until "death do you part." The dreams you brought to that relationship might include:

· your husband would always respect you
· you would have perfect children, a wonderful home, great vacations, and parties
· you would weather all storms together
· you would always have someone with whom to share experiences
· you would have a constant social companion
· you would make love endlessly
· you would be financially secure

Allow yourself to experience the sadness associated with these losses: Begin to become unstuck, unattached to these hopes and dreams so you can use your energy to develop and invest in new, more realistic hopes and dreams.

---

fell off one of the wild horses he was training and broke his leg. The neighbors said, "Guess it's a bad day." The farmer again said, "I can't say, all of my days aren't in yet." The following day war broke out and all the able-bodied young men were drafted into the service. The farmer's son couldn't go because of his broken leg.

While we might choose to label our days as good or bad, our experiences as negative or positive, all of our days aren't in yet. So, like the farmer, we might do well to greet *all* the experiences that come our way.

Darlene Moves On....

It cost her pain and hard work, but Darlene was able to see that the deaths from AIDS of so many of her friends had made her feel guilty. She had become obsessed with "should-have" thoughts: *I should have visited more, I should have given more, I should have said more.* At some level, she felt that she should have been able to save them.

> *Suffering is part of life. Moving toward mental health requires us to address to the best of our abilities the losses and disappointments we are guaranteed to experience on our journey.*

Through therapy, Darlene discovered that the feelings of guilt were easier to accept than acknowledging that, like so many things in life, these deaths were not under her control. She began to focus on coping better with the losses. One thing that helped, she found, was organizing a discussion group on HIV/AIDS at her church. "I know I can't save the world," she told me, "but doing even this little bit makes me feel better than doing nothing at all."

STEPS TO OPTIMUM MENTAL HEALTH

Suffering is part of life. Moving toward mental health requires us to address to the best of our abilities the losses and disappointments we are guaranteed to experience on our journey. Complete the exercises in this chapter to help you deal with past losses and work toward bringing a new perspective to the losses and disappointments you will face in the future.

MORE FOR YOUR HEALTH
Books

Judith Viorst: *Necessary Losses*. New York: Simon & Schuster, 1986.

Jonetta Rose Barras: *Whatever Happened to Daddy's Little Girl? The Impact of Fatherlessness on Black Women*. New York: The Ballantine Publishing Group, 2000.

Movie

Mama Flora's Family. This drama chronicles the multiple losses and challenges that a woman encounters over her lifetime.

Chapter Four

The Mouth is Smiling, But is the Heart?

Mental Illnesses Common in Black American Women

The Necessity of Facing One's Illness

How to Find Treatment for Mental Illness

Yolanda

The first time Yolanda came to my office, she was dressed in black and her attractive face bore the furrows of too many sleepless, anxious nights. Early in the session she let me know that what kept her tossing at night were questions she couldn't silence or answer: *Will they come through the door to get me? Will something happen to my children? Will my heart stop beating? Will the check bounce?* Sometimes all night long these thoughts would ring through her head like bells that wouldn't stop clanging.

Yolanda's despair settled in the room like July heat, and as I listened to her story, I knew that it was one I'd heard many times before. She was my mother, my sister, and my aunt, all the Black American women who had given and suffered greatly and whose losses outweighed their gains. As she told me her story, Yolanda shed no tears. But I could tell that she was crying inside, so loudly it echoed throughout her soul.

Yolanda's torment was rooted in the unfortunate tradition that says Black American women must be stoic and unflinching in the face of life's worst tribulation. And that reaching for help even when our sorrow is overflowing means weakness.

But Yolanda was ready to break that tradition. In fact, she had done that when she knocked on my door.

> *Depression can be as sneaky as a sucker punch: you often don't see it coming. But though it's not always easy to know you are depressed, there are early physical and mental signs of distress.*

We spend countless hours and dollars at cosmetic counters and hair and nail salons. We are putting on our faces, as the old folks would say. Yet, as the title of this chapter asks, "What is behind the mask?"

UNDERSTANDING DEPRESSION

Depression can be as sneaky as a sucker punch: you often don't see it coming. But though it's not always easy to know you are depressed, there *are* early physical and mental signs of distress. Depression may start, as Yolanda's did, with sleep problems. Or you might find yourself eating more or less, or craving certain foods like sweets or starches. You may lose interest in your usual activities. Over time, you may develop a negative outlook that you seem unable to control. Pessimistic words creep into your vocabulary. Anxiety may set in, with fear that something bad will happen to you or the people close to you. You may find yourself preoccupied with death and dying.

Depression can be hard to detect in the elderly because sometimes it is misdiagnosed as Alzheimer's. Forgetting is a common symptom for both diseases, which explains why most nursing homes screen residents carefully to insure that they are being correctly treated.

Depression is an individual problem, but it is also a social one. Health care providers are concerned that depression contributes to, and complicates, diseases like heart disease and other illnesses, and can also contribute to early deaths. More and more employers understand that depression can reduce the ability of their employees to function productively.

Depression is a highly treatable illness.

Women are twice as likely as men to experience depression during their lifetimes. Some researchers say this is the result of hormonal changes. Others attribute it to societal barriers that limit women's ability to fully reach their potential. Whatever the reason, the essential point is that depression is a highly treatable illness.

SEEING THROUGH THE MYTHS

As Black American women, we need to see through the myths that are rumored about us in our community:

- Black women don't get depressed.
- Black women don't need help to get it together.
- Black women don't attempt suicide.

If we believe in these myths, we can feel trapped and unable to seek help, because doing so may seem to confirm that we've somehow failed. The truth is, that to believe we don't have stress and distress that can eventually lead to the collapse of our coping skills is like saying we are not human. We would have to be without emotion, like Mr. Spock on the original *Star Trek* television series, whose species was incapable of feeling, and who dealt with each adventure with the cold precision of a computer.

The belief that we go through life like Spock dates back to the time when our ancestors were in chains on the plantation, and had to ignore their emotional needs in order to survive. Now, nearly 150 years since slavery was abolished, Black women continue to experience the emotional repercussions of slavery.

But I am here to say that there is no reason for us to be like Spock; we *are* human. Given the many demands of our lives, isn't it reasonable to consider that we can become "tired and worn," as the song *Precious Lord* proclaims? Many of us have been "tired and worn" for a long time, but have been reluctant to believe that this feeling may actually be depression.

BODY PAIN AND DEPRESSION

People who don't know they are depressed sometimes experience physical symptoms (such as chronic headaches, diarrhea, heart palpitations, or abdominal or back pain), for which the doctor cannot find a cause.

A high percentage of people with chronic pain suffer from depression and people with depression often report that they feel pain (sometimes termed "masked depression"). When the

DEPRESSION SYMPTOM CHECKLIST*

Read the following list, copy it, and check those symptoms that apply to you. Bring the list to your health care provider on your first visit to her. Checking a particular symptom doesn't mean you have depression, but because many depression symptoms overlap with other illnesses, this information can be useful to your physician.

Check all the symptoms that apply:

___ I am often restless and irritable

___ I am having irregular sleep patterns--either too much or not enough

___ I don't enjoy hobbies, my friends, family, or leisure activities any more

___ I am having trouble managing my diabetes, hypertension, or other chronic illness

___ I have nagging aches and pains that do not get better no matter what I do. Specifically, I often experience:

☐ Digestive problems

☐ Headache or backache

☐ Vague aches and pains like joint or muscle pains

☐ Chest pains

☐ Dizziness

___ I have trouble concentrating or making simple decisions

___ Others have commented on my mood or attitude lately

___ My weight has changed a considerable amount

___ I have had several of the symptoms I checked above for more than two weeks

___ I feel that my functioning in everyday life (work, family, friends) is suffering because of these problems

___ I have a family history of depression

___ I have thought about suicide

* Adapted from the University of Michigan Depression Center Symptom Checklist

main symptoms are fatigue along with disturbance of the normal sleep and eating patterns, a person's condition is labeled "somatic depression." Silverstein found that women, and especially Black women, are more likely to suffer from somatic depression, and, in particular, somatic depression with anxiety.[15]

Researchers looking at Black Americans and White Americans in the primary medical care setting found a difference in the severity of somatic symptoms reported.[16] Dr. Fran Baker, in a study of older African Americans, found that Black women were more likely to report symptoms of anger, irritability, and denial of illness, and to spontaneously report somatic complaints rather than symptoms that reflected a change in mood.[17]

In the movie, *Imitiation of Life,* the Black housekeeper takes to her bed when her daughter disowns her in order to pass for White. This is a wonderful example of how psychological loss or grief leads us to physical symptoms. In the African-American community, complaining of physical symptoms is more acceptable than admitting to mental distress.

While the final evidence isn't in on the cause of major depression and other mood disorders, we do know that often, during postpartum, premenstrual, and menopausal times, mood disorders can be intense. Fluctuations and changes in the level of estrogen affect other chemicals that modulate our ability to handle stress, and may put us at greater risk for depression.

Other factors that may cause or contribute to depression include medical conditions such as diabetes, stroke, HIV/AIDS, and thyroid conditions. In addition, certain medications—such as steroids used for asthma or birth control pills—may contribute to depression.

The following is a more complete, but by no means inclusive, list of depressive symptoms:

- depressed mood or loss of interest or pleasure that goes on for two weeks or more
- significant weight loss or weight gain
- sleeplessness or sleeping too much
- significantly increased or decreased motor activity (psychomotor agitation or retardation)
- fatigue or loss of energy
- feelings of worthlessness or excessive or inappropriate guilt
- diminished ability to think or concentrate, indecisiveness
- hopelessness
- recurrent thoughts of death or suicide

Some of these emotions are natural during the worst periods of bereavement or other crisis. But when they don't go away, you need to look at them, with the help of a person trained in psychological counseling.

A common form of mental illness is known as manic-depressive illness or bipolar disorder. The term "bipolar" refers to the two extremes that the individual experiences. When up, or manic, the person experiences an elevated sense of one's self and one's situation. The person may spend more money than she actually has, become involved in many projects and activities, some of them very big and unrealistic.

The other side of bipolar disorder is depression. In this phase, a person's sense of self is marked by negativity. A person who hits the bottom of depression may experience herself as the lowest human being ever born, and may be unable to view

Symptoms of Mania
· frequent or constant irritability
· inflated self-esteem (grandiosity)
· decreased need for sleep
· extreme talkativeness
· racing thoughts or flights of ideas (rapid shift from one idea to another)
· distractibility
· increased goal-directed activity or physical agitation
· excessive involvement in pleasurable activities that have a high potential for painful consequences.[18]

life positively. The job, marriage, a friend, a child, or music that once gave great pleasure now can't touch the core of gloom into which a deeply depressed person's self has sunk.

SPECIALIZED CLASSES OF DEPRESSION

Here are a few more specialized classes of depression that may help you understand the problem further:

Dysthymic Disorder is a depression, usually mild or moderate, that lasts for at least two years. People with dysthymic disorder may have periods of normal mood that last for up to two months, but they generally are depressed more days than not during those years.

Postpartum Depression is a disorder that has its onset within four weeks of delivery of a child.

Seasonal Affective Disorder usually involves a depression that begins in the fall and/or winter and ends in the spring. Sixty to ninety percent of patients diagnosed with this disorder are women.

MENTAL DISORDERS DUE TO
A MEDICAL CONDITION

Mental disorders are sometimes the result of a physical illness. At some time during most people's lives, they or someone they know will experience disorientation because of sickness. Something as simple as a fever or as complex as a seizure can cause confusion. People with liver failure because of alcohol abuse have been known to exhibit disorientation and even to be out of touch with reality. Delirium is particularly frequent among hospitalized patients. Medical conditions can also lead to elevation or depression of mood, or manifest themselves as irritability.

Diabetes is a disease to which Black Americans should pay special attention, because of its prevalence in our community. Over 2.2 million Black Americans have diabetes. For every six White Americans who have diabetes, ten Black Americans have it. In every age group, more Black American women have diabetes than Black American men. Black Americans are twice as likely as White Americans to die from diabetes.

Some studies have found that forty percent of diabetics also have clinical depression. Either disease can strike first. Women who are depressed may give up exercising and overeat to the point of developing diabetes. Women who already have diabetes may develop depression. Depression adversely effects how the body responds to insulin. Diabetics who are depressed are more likely to be lax in following the treatment recommended by their physicians. The cumulative impact of depression and diabetes may be heart and kidney disease and early death.

As I mentioned earlier, steroids, correctly used for several ailments, may clog the engine of mental functioning. High doses or rapid changes in the dose can lead to psychosis, where you aren't sure what is real and what is not.

ANXIETY DISORDERS
Sheila

Sheila knew exactly what her problem was: she had a heart condition. She knew it was her heart because when she awoke in the middle of the night, it would be pounding furiously like it was trying to beat its way out of her body. She would be short of breath and the bed would be soaked from her sweat. She was certain her heart was going to kill her and it would happen on the highway and the ambulance wouldn't make it on time. So she stopped driving on the highway.

But three emergency room visits and examinations by as many doctors showed that nothing was wrong with Sheila. The doctors told her she was simply stressed out. "Yes, I'm stressed, but something is definitely wrong," she told me, hoping I could help her. During our first session, I learned that Sheila's "heart troubles" began two months after her second child was born. We were able to trace a link between Sheila's heart troubles and her anxiety.

Anxiety disorders are among the most common ailments with which Black American women live. Anxiety can present itself in a host of ways, as short, discrete episodes or as an ongoing condition. It may be associated with specific events or even specific objects, like bridges—or it may have no identifiable cause.

Most clinicians distinguish anxiety from fear. Fear comes from a perceived external danger, while anxiety is seen as having an internal source.

A panic attack is a specific anxiety disorder that usually involves considerable discomfort. Some researchers have found that the rate of suicide among people suffering from panic disorders may be as high as among people with major depression. Sometimes panic disorders are triggered or made worse by the loss of an important interpersonal relationship.

Fear comes from a perceived external danger, while anxiety is seen as having an internal source.

Panic disorders occur more frequently in women than in men and are not uncommon among women who have given birth. Researchers offer theories about a possible hormonal relationship.

Here are some common anxiety disorders and their common symptoms:

Panic Disorder
- intense apprehension, fearfulness, or terror, often associated with feelings of impending doom
- shortness of breath, palpitations, chest pain or discomfort, choking or smothering sensations
- fear of going crazy or losing control
- Agoraphobia. A person may have anxiety about, or

avoidance of, places and situations from which escape might be perceived as difficult or embarrassing, or in which help may not be available in the event of a panic attack

Specific Phobia

Significant anxiety provoked by exposure to a specific feared object or situation. This anxiety often leads to avoidance behavior.

Social Phobia

Anxiety provoked by certain types of social or performance situations. This anxiety commonly causes the person to avoid the associated situation.

Obsessive-Compulsive Disorder

- Obsessions, which cause marked anxiety or distress, and/or compulsions, which serve to neutralize anxiety.
- *Obsessions* include thoughts, ideas, impulses, and images that are intrusive and inappropriate, about contamination, doubts, the order of things, aggressive or horrific impulses, and sexual imagery. Concerns include thoughts not usually related to real life problems.
- *Compulsions* are repetitive thoughts or behaviors such as checking the door, hand washing, praying, counting, or repeating words, done with the goal of preventing and reducing anxiety or distress. The person feels driven to perform these actions to reduce the distress that accompanies an obsession or to prevent some perceived dreaded event or situation.

Post Traumatic Stress Disorder (PTSD)

This disorder follows direct personal experience of an event that involves actual or threatened death or serious injury. It is expected to be experienced by many people who were directly or indirectly involved in the 9/11/2001 tragedies. A PTSD response involves:

- persistent re-experiencing of an extremely traumatic event
- intense fear, helplessness, or horror
- avoidance of stimuli associated with the trauma
- numbing of general responsiveness
- duration of at least one month
- impairment in functioning
- attempts to avoid thoughts, feelings, or conversations about the event
- amnesia for important aspects of the trauma
- markedly reduced ability to feel emotions (especially those associated with intimacy, tenderness, sexuality)
- sense of foreshortened future
- impaired ability to handle affects (feelings)

This disorder may be particularly severe if it results from torture or rape. There may be associated feelings of shame, despair, hopelessness, and guilt about being a survivor.

Acute Stress Disorder

Like PTSD, but occurs within four weeks of the event and resolves itself during that four-week period.

PSYCHOTIC DISORDERS
Tiffany

The police who brought Tiffany into the emergency room had done it so many times that it had become a routine. One night, they found her lying in the middle of the street. She told whoever would listen that she was going to die soon. She had stopped taking her anti-psychotic medication so the voice in her head had gotten worse. She told the ER staff that the voice came from a cruel man who controlled her thoughts and actions.

She was determined to get rid of that man by ending her life.

There are many stereotypes about individuals suffering from a mental illness:

- They are out of control.
- They are homeless.
- They are filthy.
- They are violent and don't care who they hurt.

Extreme cases are the ones that get media attention and are probably to blame for the generally false profiles. The reality is that *people with mental illness are no more likely to be violent than people who do not have mental disorders. They are more frequently a danger to themselves than to others.*

Psychosis can be associated with mood disorders and schizophrenia. *Psychotic* means out of touch with reality: a psychotic person no longer has the ability to distinguish between what is real and what isn't. Someone who is severely psychotic may hear voices and experience delusions (that is, false beliefs, such as believing you are the devil or that others are out to harm you).

Schizophrenia is a term we use when a patient has two or more of the following symptoms during a one-month period:

- delusions
- hallucinations
- disorganized speech

In addition, a person with schizophrenia may experience grossly disorganized or catatonic behavior, lack feeling, and be unable to work effectively on the job or in social situations.

Schizophrenia is not caused by other disorders (for example, mood disorders or substance abuse).

Hearing a patient complain that she hears voices should not automatically lead a mental health clinician to diagnose the patient with schizophrenia. The far too frequent diagnosis of schizophrenia in Black Americans has been a concern among mental health practitioners.

A woman I know, call her Jane, complained to her doctor that she was depressed. and distrusted strangers. She was labeled paranoid. What the doctor seemed not to know is that, for many African Americans, distrust of strangers is a necessary and useful coping skill. Lately, increased attention has been given to race-based misdiagnoses by training providers to be more sensitive to cultural differences. Psychosis does exist, and the experience of being psychotic can be intensely distressing. The voices and delusions are frightening. The rate of suicide for people with schizophrenia approaches that of those with depression. People who suffer chronic hallucinations and delusions may find their symptoms too much to bear. Imagine believing that everyone is against you, even your family and friends, or that all your food is poisoned. It is like being imprisoned, with your own ill mind as the warden.

Psychotic symptoms can sometimes result from medications or their withdrawal. People who are too quickly taken off steroids or who are withdrawing from alcohol may experience psychotic symptoms.

EATING DISORDERS

It is estimated that a third of the population of the United States is obese; the number is thought to be higher among Black American women. Eating disorders included in the *Diagnostic and Statistical Manual of Mental Disorders* include anorexia nervosa and bulimia nervosa. Obesity is not included because it has not been firmly established that it is consistently associated with a set of behavioral or psychological symptoms. But while it is not listed separately as a disorder, it can be a symptom of depression and in itself can cause stress and depression.

Anorexia Nervosa
- refusal to maintain body weight at or above a minimally normal weight for age and height
- intense fear of gaining weight or becoming fat, even though underweight
- disturbance in the way one's body weight or shape is experienced or denial of the seriousness of the current low body weight
- missed period for three consecutive cycles in young women who had started menses

Bulimia Nervosa

- recurrent episodes of binge eating
- recurrent, inappropriate compensatory behavior to prevent weight gain: self-induced vomiting, misuse of laxatives, diuretics, enemas
- binge eating and inappropriate compensatory behaviors both occur, on average, at least twice a week for three months
- self-evaluation is unduly influenced by body shape and weight

SUICIDE

Tanya

Tanya believed her death had already occurred. All that needed to be planned now was disposal of her remains. Her dying had come gradually, over a long period of time. It began with the disconnection from the people she loved and cared for. It announced itself each Sunday when she stopped going to church. It displayed itself when she no longer combed her hair and stopped covering up the gray. The depression was there when she wore the same black dress so many times the hem fell out and she was too tired to repair it. The phone went unanswered, the bills went unpaid, and she was too numb to even cry. So it didn't feel like suicide when she took the pills. It just felt like completing what had been started a long time ago.

Attempting or committing suicide is often the result of despair. It rarely happens out of the blue. Usually it becomes an option after a long period of hopelessness, during which time help is no longer perceived as available. It is self-annihilation, but to someone who has suffered long-term, suicide seems the only option to overwhelming agony. Of the 30,000 suicides a year in the United States, it is believed that most are committed by people who have a diagnosable mental disorder.

The goal of diagnosing depression before it becomes severe is to prevent premature death and disability. Severe depression can lead you to the point where you are no longer able to think rationally about your condition. Your thoughts and plans are distorted by a negative world view. Successful suicides are estimated to be as high as fifteen to twenty percent in people who are depressed. Mental health providers want to catch depression as early as possible before suicide becomes a serious option.

For years, suicide rates in the Black American community have been low, but this reality has changed. Dr. Alvin Pouissant and Amy Alexander note in *Lay My Burden Down,* their powerful study of suicide and mental health among Black Americans, that the suicide rate for young Black American men has risen dramatically over the past twenty years, as the result of a loss of hope.[19] The rates for Black American women, however, have been historically low and continue to be lower than the rates for other groups. Some people believe those low figures can be attributed to our spirituality. At the same time, while suicide rates are low, researchers and clinicians are looking at other harmful behaviors that Black American women direct towards themselves—such as over-eating, lack of exercise, substance abuse, and unprotected sex.

Suicide doesn't always occur as a result of long-term planning. For some individuals overwhelmed by a recent event, such as the breakup of a relationship, unemployment, or a terminal diagnosis, suicide may be seen as an acceptable solution. This final act allows them to feel some sense of control. Alcohol and drugs have given people the courage to attempt, or succeed at, killing themselves.

If depression is treated early, or panic disorders and the distressing symptoms of schizophrenia are controlled, and they can be, people do not have to get to the point of self-injurious behavior.

It is also worth noting that fifty percent of people who commit suicide use a gun. We must address the issue of protecting ourselves and our loved ones from using weapons self-destructively. Too often, the same weapons somebody purchased for protection end up doing just the opposite.

Here are some other mental illnesses that we should be aware of, as described in the *Diagnostic and Statistical Manual of Mental Disorder:*

Somatoform Disorder
- the patient has physical symptoms (for example, paralysis or pain) that can't be explained fully by a medical diagnosis.
- the patient may be preoccupied with having a serious condition because of misinterpreting body function or symptoms

Impulse-Control Disorder
- The patient fails to resist the impulse, drive, or temptation to perform an act that is harmful to herself or other people.

- The patient feels an increased sense of tension or arousal before committing the act and then experiences pleasure, gratification or relief at the time of committing it.
- The patient may or may not experience regret, self-reproach or guilt.

Intermittent Explosive Disorder

This condition is a failure to resist aggressive impulses, resulting in serious assaults or destruction of property.

Kleptomania

This condition involves a failure to resist impulses to steal objects not needed for personal use or monetary value.

Pyromania

This condition involves setting fires for pleasure.

Pathological Gambling

This condition involves recurrent and persistent maladaptive gambling behavior.

Sexual Disorders

These are disorders of sexual functioning that may involve desire, arousal, orgasm, or pain.

Substance Abuse/Dependence Disorders

- abuse involves the recurrent use of substances despite adverse consequences. There may be physical, legal, interpersonal, and social effects.
- dependence involves symptoms that occur with use

despite serious problems. The person develops tolerance to the substance and needs more to get the same effect.

Learning Disorders

These are disorders involving reading, math, or written expression.

Attention-Deficit/Hyperactivity

- persistent pattern of inattention and/or hyperactivity-impulsivity that is more frequent and severe than is typically observed in individuals at a comparable level of development
- occurs in academic, occupational, social spheres
- difficulty completing tasks
- avoidance of activities that demand sustained mental effort and require close attention
- fidgetiness, squirming, excessive running
- impulsiveness

WHEN HELP IS NEEDED

In brief, you need help from mental health services when you simply can't cope. Not being able to cope may mean being unable to handle family tasks, inability to go to work, and even, in some cases, inability to get out of bed. It means that you've lost the capacity to experience and enjoy your ordinary life, and you feel overwhelmed by negative emotions and ideas.

People who have gone through such an experience express a host of feelings and thoughts about it. Some people express shame about being so out of control; others report fear and anxiety about this loss of control occurring again, or becoming constant. Still others have few emotions they are willing to share and limit their involvement in aftercare services in the community.

Aftercare services include a psychotherapist and someone who will continue to monitor the prescribed psychiatric medicines. These services can help prevent women from deteriorating to the point that they can no longer work or have gratifying relationships, it can keep them from stays in hospitals or clinics, and it can help others from having to return to the hospital.

Some people may experience many psychiatric admissions and periods when their coping skills fail because of acute illness. When it has been necessary for them to be involuntarily hospitalized, they are often angry with family members, mental health professionals, and authorities in law enforcement and the courts who were responsible for having them committed.

People with mental disorders are not always acutely ill. They may have long periods when their symptoms decrease in severity or even vanish. A person with schizophrenia may have times when her hallucinations or delusions are under control. Those with manic-depressive illness may experience long periods when they are symptom-free. Others may have several cycles of depressions and mania over the course of a year.

During the acute phase of these illnesses, there may be episodes that are particularly embarrassing to the individual. The person may engage in excessive spending and write bad checks, disrobe in the throes of a delusion, or destroy property. Once the person is stabilized, she has to come to terms with what has happened. This process takes a lot of courage and support from her mental health care provider and from the people who care about her.

It needs courage to come to terms with a breakdown, to tell yourself that you've lost your last nerve. But you can find that courage by accepting the reality that you are overwhelmed. Once you have accepted this reality, you can take some deep breaths and begin to sort out what was and what was not under your control.

We talk throughout this book about how you can change things that *are* in your control. But it is essential to remember that biology is important in determining our mental health. That's why you need a good physical examination when you begin to cope with a breakdown. Sometimes people suffer severe breakdowns because they've taken themselves off medication without consulting their doctors. To do that is to play with fire.

With the help of your doctor and a psychotherapist, you can learn about the cause of your illness and how it works, and you can then begin to direct your energy toward what is under your control. You will need to eliminate the stress that can be eliminated and learn to cope with stress that can't.

Families can become overwhelmed by the impact mental illness of one member has on their lives but, out of family loyalty, they struggle on. Yet the family must be able to recognize when they can no longer care for that person at home. It is at this point where the family may be obliged to seek an emergency petition, which allows the police to escort the sick person, without that person's permission or agreement, to an emergency room for a mental health evaluation. At times, however we may regret it, this is the only way to insure that the loved one will receive a psychiatric evaluation and, if needed, the hospitalization required to prevent her from harming herself or others. The need for an emergency petition often arises because the patient has waited too long in denial. Perhaps she is suffering long-range sleep or appetite disturbance, and feeling constantly stressed out. Yet she's sure she can pull herself together, and others around her may encourage that belief.

Fear of seeking help or fear that other people will think she is crazy or weak may cause a woman to struggle on, past the point when mild symptoms could have been treated easily. Left unattended, those same mild symptoms of depression can lead to a person's inability to work or take care of herself, or even, eventually, to suicidal thoughts and actions. At that time, someone else must step in. How much better to face the trouble early and nip it in the bud.

People are often uneasy in the company of people who have at some time lost control of their mental functioning. They are concerned because they see the individual as being unpredictable. Lay people need to understand that such loss of control can be extremely frightening for the individual experiencing it. Delusions of persecution (where one believes others will harm her) are particularly frightening. That's why it is important to get the patient to a secure place such as an emergency room, where the staff knows how to assure the patient that she will not be harmed and prevent her from harming others.

For Black Americans, it's well to keep in mind that our reluctance to seek help means that when we finally do get it we're likely to be in crisis. The pot boils over before people are willing to acknowledge a flame is on. If people would be less ready to say, "I don't need a shrink! I'm not crazy!" they would be more likely to find good counseling at the right time—*before* they become overwhelmed by the stress of life.

A final note: often, the psychotherapist you visit also will have experienced therapy and explored issues from her own past. This means that she will be especially sensitive to your issues because she may have struggled with them herself.

Yolanda Moves On....

Yolanda returned for follow-up three weeks after starting an antidepressant. She wore red now, and reported her sleep and appetite were back to normal. She was planning to return to church that Sunday after having missed several weeks because of her depression. She felt she was getting back to herself.

Sheila Moves On....

It took Sheila several more trips to the emergency room before she was willing to accept a diagnosis of panic disorder. The doctors prescribed antidepressants to help prevent attacks, along with antianxiety medication that would provide immediate relief should an attack occur. Sheila was also referred to an anxiety specialist who helped her learn deep breathing techniques to decrease the severity and duration of her attacks. She was eventually eased off the antianxiety medication, but continued with the antidepressant.

Tiffany Moves On....

Doctors re-started Tiffany on antipsychotic and antidepressant medications. But after discharge from the hospital, she stopped taking her medicine. During my tenure at the hospital, she was admitted several times with hallucinations that told her to harm herself. Multiple medications, including mood stabilizers, were used, but Tiffany gained little insight into the need for taking the long-term medication she needed to prevent hospitalization.

STEPS TO OPTIMUM MENTAL HEALTH

Each year, the National Mental Health Association sponsors National Depression Screening Day in October, and National Anxiety Screening Day in May. You can call the MNHA Resource Center at 800–969–6642 for specific dates and the names of participating mental health providers in your area.

MORE FOR YOUR HEALTH
Book

Meri Nana-Ama Danquah: *Willow Weep for Me*. New York: W W Norton & Company, 1998.

Movies

Imitation of Life. Shows how depression can shorten one's life.
A Beautiful Mind. Reveals the painstaking experience of mental illness.
The Caveman's Valentine. Shows a Black American man's experience with psychosis.

CHAPTER FIVE

MAKING PREPARATIONS DOES NOT SPOIL THE TRIP

Creating a Life Management Plan

Tonya

Tonya was a thirty-eight-year-old single woman being treated for depression. For the past five years, she had spent Mother's Day in the psychiatric unit of her local hospital. When her mother died suddenly six years ago, they weren't speaking. Tonya attended only part of the wake before she became overwhelmed and left the service. She couldn't visit the burial site. Each year, as she got closer to the anniversary of her mother's death, she developed sleeping problems. It took her a while to fall asleep, and then she had nightmares about her endless arguments with her mother. When she over-ate, she often imagined her mother's negative comments.

Tonya had attempted suicide each year around the time of Mother's Day by taking an overdose of her high blood pressure medication.

Dr. Hans Selye, an expert on stress, defines stress as "mental or physical effects of any demands upon the body."[20] Along with that clinical definition should be photographs of every Black American woman in the country, because each of us could write our own book about stress. The phrase "stressless woman" is an oxymoron. The two words contradict one another.

Here's a familiar picture. It's Monday morning, you've been up most of the night putting the finishing touches on a report due at 9 a.m., and you've slept longer than you should have. After shouting at your teenage daughter a half dozen times to hurry out of the bathroom, you finally get in. There's barely enough hot water for a shower. You're putting on your makeup when you smell something burning downstairs. Your ten-year-old son left the bacon in the microwave and he's fanning the smoldering remains in the kitchen sink. You look at the clock: you've got ten minutes to get the kids in the car. Attached to the refrigerator is a note from your husband, a reminder that he won't be home for dinner. He's working late again. Getting your son to school, you get ticketed for running a stop sign, and just as you drop him off, you remember that you left that report on your desk at home. It's as if the whole universe had begun to turn against you, and you wonder, "Why me?"

For many of us, life is similar to doing hard time. Like prisoners on a chain gang, day in and day out, we are driven by raw survival. We saw our mothers and grandmothers do their time, and believe our lot will be the same. No hope for release now, no hope for it later.

Doing hard time requires a lot of toughness, and we imagine that we have plenty of that. Aren't we all Super Black

Women? But that image, as I've said, is as much a curse as it is a blessing. It drives us to meet our obligations and to produce, but along with keeping us busy, it keeps us numb enough to shut out the inner voices of pain, rejection, and rage.

We cannot escape from our prison until we acknowledge we are prisoners. Too often, the truth of our suffering is sometimes only apparent to others who are doing the same thing, *fronting* just like us.

> *We cannot escape from our prison until we acknowledge we are prisoners.*

Facing the truth means swallowing a bitter pill: the demands life makes on us, which we sometimes experience as stress, are a fact of life. We'll only stop experiencing stress after death, although some people might say they will have to deal with stress on the other side.

While we're here on earth, our bodies and minds seek to be in a state of balance called "homeostasis." Everything that requires a reaction on our part may be considered stressful. Psychologists distinguish between two kinds of stress: the positive ones are called *eustress* and the negative ones are called, more familiarly, *distress*. We experience eustress when we rise to meet demands, and distress when we crumble beneath them.

The Serenity Prayer is an essential stress management tool. In it, you are asking a Higher Power to help you to accept the things you cannot change, the courage to change the things you can, and the wisdom to know the difference. In Chapter Three, we focused on the things we cannot change—losses, disappointments, and failures that have accompanied us on our trip through life. Successful grieving has to do with accepting and honoring the lessons and blessings they have provided us. Stress management involves identifying the events and circumstances we have some ability to affect or manage.

People with recurrent mental illnesses, such as psychosis or depression, often have a stressful factor that contributes to their relapse. The stress may be one that they are conscious of, but it may also be an event they have put out of their awareness, such as the anniversary of the death of a loved one. This pattern can show itself in other forms of destructive behavior just short of breakdown. People who go on and off diets often point to a stressful event or feeling which played a part in their return to unhealthy foods or overeating.

SAVING OUR LAST NERVE

Nowhere in this book is the phrase "saving our last nerve" more important—because here is where I speak directly about how you can avoid becoming one of the case histories in this chapter. The trick is to help yourself *before* you lose it totally and need help .

An excellent starting point is the journal you should have already started to keep. Now you may want to expand it. Your journal can provide you with the kind of dialogue you might experience in therapy. In therapy, you learn to observe your thoughts and behaviors and, where you wish to change them, decide whether you are willing to take some action to bring your thoughts and behavior under your control.

You can explore some of that process in the journal itself. As a first step, take the time and make the effort to reflect on troublesome thoughts and behavior as they occur in the course of a particular day. At first, such reflection may take some conscious practice and determination. Often we are so caught up in experiencing things that we forget about this other part of our mind—the observing ego that can be quite useful to us.

Once you have gotten into the habit of keeping your journal, you can begin to develop a Life or Stress Management Plan. The goal here is really simple: to get a clear picture of what you are truly able to do, as opposed to what you are desperately trying to do.

You'll have to evaluate your present activities objectively. Should you really preside over Women's Day at church when you have already agreed to be on the PTA committee, work on the Delta's annual conference, and monitor homework for three children? Is now the best time to start that new class? Does driving your husband to work in the morning, along with getting the children off to school, keep you from getting any control of your morning? So list the things you do, and perhaps start asking yourself which of them you might possibly give up to make your life easier. You are now ready for a stress screen.

Stress Screen

To help yourself begin to manage the stresses in your life, ask yourself the following questions and record your answers in your journal:

- Do you frequently feel you are losing control?
- Have you noticed ongoing changes in your appetite or sleeping?

- Are you easily irritated?
- Do you frequently worry about your finances or other concerns?
- Have you had major life changes over the past six months? For example, a move, a divorce, loss or change of a job, the birth of a child.
- Have you had medical problems recently?
- Are you experiencing frequent headaches or back pains or muscle tension?
- Are you having difficulty concentrating, making decisions, or forgetting things?
- Have you increased your use of alcohol or other drugs?
- Have you experienced a racing heart rate, shortness of breath or nervousness?
- Are you having muscle twitches, heartburn, or excessive sweating?
- Do you often feel overwhelmed?

If you answer "yes" to several of these questions, you may want to have a more formal screen by your physician, who can help make sure that medical conditions are not the cause of the problem.

As you begin to recognize the causes of stress in your life, deal first with those that have bothered you recently. In your journal, include your reflections on how you deal with them. Gradually, you may find that some of these stresses have been with you for a long time, and they will probably remain with you for a longer time unless you find a way of coping.

Once you begin to recognize and understand your stress patterns, you are ready to develop a stress management plan

SAMPLE SELF-ANALYSIS OF STRESS REACTIONS

Stress Reaction	*Outcome*
Fight with partner	drank several margaritas had headache and felt worse
Hard day at work	rode bicycle felt mentally better and glad I exercised
Received high gas bill	ate four slices of pizza felt angry with myself

that truly works for you by making your life simpler and more manageable. Your Stress Management Plan begins by listing areas, or categories you need to think about, along with the specific ways you mean to work in this area, and how often each day or week.

Once you have put these categories in your notebook, either copied or pasted in from this book, make a daily calendar numbered one to twelve, and for each day record which of these activities you were involved in and, specifically, how. Put in a sentence or two about how it felt.

There are several areas you should include when developing your plan to Save Your Last Nerve. Your goal is to manage the demands that are put on you with the least amount of discomfort and to increase the satisfaction you experience in your life. You will want to have activities you do daily, weekly, monthly, every six months and yearly.

Here's an example of how the details might look in your notebook:

STRESS MANAGEMENT PLAN

Area	*Activity*	*Frequency*
1. Relaxation		
2. Physical Activity		
3. Anger/Frustration		
4. Support System		
5. Prioritizing/Time Pressures		
6. Organization		
7. Spirituality/ Values		
8. Humor		
9. Nutrition		
10. Medications		
11. Rewards/ Affirmations		
12. Therapy		

MY STRESS MANAGEMENT PLAN

Area	Activity	Frequency
1. Relaxation	deep breathing exercise	twice daily and as needed
	20 minutes meditation	daily
	walk labyrinth	2x/month
2. Physical Activity	walk 2 miles	4x/week
3. Anger/ Frustration	journal	when frustrated/ angry
	assertiveness training	listen to audio tape two times
4. Support System	talk to sister or girlfriend	daily
	private time with partner	2x/week
5. Prioritizing/ Time	complete my daily to do list	daily
	set goals for the week	Sunday night
	set goals for the year	each birthday
6. Organization	get rid of junk mail, old clothes, toys	weekly
7. Values/ Spirituality	pray	daily and as needed
	attend church	weekly
	work in spiritual development book	every other week
8. Humor	attend comedy club	1x/year
	read comics	every weekend
	read joke book	3x/year
9. Nutrition	consult doctor on best nutritional plan for me	1 visit
	stick to plan	daily work
10. Medications	antidepressant	daily
	antihypertensive	daily
	nutritional supplement	daily
11. Rewards/ Affirmation	massage	every six weeks
	weekend getaway	every four months
	new perfume	when you reach new weight goal
	positive feedback	at least 3/day
12. Therapy support	group for survivors of abuse	weekly

Remember that increased physical activity is an important component. Realistically, few of us are exactly at ideal body weight, but don't use this fact as an excuse to give up. As long as your doctor gives the go ahead, try to increase your physical activity just a little bit at a time. The goal is to help your body and mind function better.

If money is a subject that stresses you, you might try bartering. If you have a friend who gives massages, see if she will give one in exchange for watching her children for a few hours.

The public library is a good resource for tapes and books. There is literature available on success techniques, anger management, stress management, assertiveness training, and how to deal with difficult people. There are also tapes to teach relaxation, tai chi, massage—tapes on just about anything you would like to learn how to do.

Don't forget pleasures you engaged in when you were younger but put aside, such as knitting, cooking, listening to music, or going to church.

In terms of personal time, check out spiritual centers in your area. They often have low-cost accommodations where you can have your own retreat or participate in an organized one.

Remember, this is not a dress rehearsal—let yourself experience the pleasure of your current life. If you can't, seriously think about getting help to discover why you won't let yourself experience the joy life has to offer.

Why are we trying to do so much anyway? Over-committing ourselves can be seen as a form of self-abuse. We set ourselves up to be overstressed and then, when we can't finish what we started, we verbally abuse ourselves for not accomplishing what was probably impossible from the beginning.

METHODS OF COPING WITH STRESS

Tracking how you have handled demands gives you an opportunity to consider using new means of addressing them now or in the future. Sometimes, we turn to margaritas or pizza simply because we can't think of anything else to do. We need new tools in our bag of tricks. Here are some methods for dealing with stress that you might want to consider using.

Breathing

Sure, you've been breathing all your life. My question is, when things go wrong, are you breathing right? The primary goal of breathing is to supply our bodies with needed oxygen. When we are stressed, the demand for oxygen increases, as does our rate of breathing, but the depth of breath decreases.

Deep breathing, also called diaphragmatic breathing (breathing with focus on the diaphragm—a muscle that separates our lungs from our abdomen,) also called deep breathing, helps to slow down your breathing and calm you. It can lower your blood pressure and heart rate, and relax muscles. This type of breathing allows your diaphragm muscle to drop down, which allows more space for your lungs to expand. By expanding, your lungs can give to your body the extra oxygen it needs during times of stress.

One method of exercising your diaphragm and getting control over it is called the "button exercise." Sit or lie comfortably in a quiet place. Take a deep breath and, while doing so, imagine you are wearing a tight pair of pants. Your goal is to expand your stomach enough to pop the button off. Then exhale as you allow your abdomen to relax. As you do this several times, you should find yourself more relaxed. This is an exercise you can practice several times a day for at least ten minutes.

Meditation

Yes, Black Americans *do* meditate. Although meditation isn't popular with us, there are more of us doing it. It is a superb stress management technique that has been around for centuries. The singer Tina Turner said during a *60 Minutes* interview that meditation was responsible for rescuing her from an abusive and dangerous relationship, and helped keep her star shining bright. Meditation, done properly, leads to a sense of tranquility and enlightenment. As if all that weren't enough, meditation has also been shown to lower blood pressure, decrease the release of the stress hormones norepinephrine and cortisol, and increase mental clarity.

To begin meditating you need to find a quiet comfortable place to sit. The general technique of meditation involves focusing on a word, sound, or your breath. Close your eyes and slowly focus on your deep breathing techniques. Once you are focused on your breathing, you may wish to repeat a special word, or mantra, at your own pace. You could use the word *peace, one, Lord*, or any word that is special to you.

As you begin, you may notice other thoughts creeping in to your mind; we are busy women with a lot on our minds. Notice the presence of your thoughts, but return to your word, your mantra. Don't struggle *not* to think. Just watch these thoughts come and go, and always return to your word, your mantra and your breathing. Practice this technique for fifteen to twenty minutes each day. You may find that it works so well for you that soon you'll want to sit for half an hour each day.

Many meditation and relaxation tapes are available in bookstores. Some include guided imagery that explains how to train your mind to develop relaxing images.

The Importance of Exercise

Unfortunately, for many Black women, exercise seems unfeminine. Some find the idea threatening. For others, it threatens to mess up a new hairstyle. So it's time for a reality pill: regular exercise makes your body and mind healthier. Everyone who exercises regularly will agree to that. Further, people who exercise have a lower incidence of heart disease and diabetes. Finally, exercise is an excellent treatment for depression.

I've heard all the reasons for not exercising, and I know that they are sometimes real, or, at least, seem real until you have decided to get past them. Maybe you are afraid it will be expensive. It's true that membership in a YMCA or health club can run to $30.00 or more a month. It's also true that you might need a little equipment.

But keep in mind that just walking vigorously is excellent exercise. All you need is a good pair of shoes and clothes that protect you in all kinds of weather. If you don't like walking in the rain or snow, find a nearby mall. If you don't like walking alone, recruit a friend, or join a friend who already has the good habit of walking.

Some people say "I'm just not in shape to exercise." Maybe you're not, but everyone can do something. Start off walking to the corner and back. Soon it will be easy to walk around the block. You'll be surprised to find how quickly you'll be doing a thirty-minute walk without trouble. In fact, that walk may be a high point of your day.

Of course, if you have any medical condition that might limit your exercise program, talk to your doctor. But he will be able to recommend some level of exercise that you can participate in.

If your own neighborhood doesn't feel safe for exercises like walking, take a bus to one that does feel safe and walk there. You deserve to feel good about your life. You deserve to feel healthy in body and mind. So tell yourself just that: I deserve the benefits of exercise, just as all other human beings do.

Sometimes our resistance to exercise is grounded in problems of self-esteem. Because we don't value ourselves, we also don't value the body that houses our soul. When you don't exercise, though the doctor recommends it and your stress management program requires it, you're "dissing" the very vessel so crucial to your time on earth. You may say, "I'm too busy," but if you look closely at the problem, with the help of your journal, you may find it's a self-esteem issue. If we dislike or don't respect ourselves, we will not take actions to help ourselves. (If you are getting stuck, read about self-esteem in Chapter Six.)

Choosing Your Exercise

After getting the okay from your physician, your first step is to choose an activity that you will enjoy and that will be most convenient for you. You have already read about the benefits of walking. If you live or work in a building with steps, consider tackling at least one flight a day. Going up and down stairs might be challenging at first, but our bodies develop endurance and strength with repetition, so hang in there. Soon you will be able to accomplish more without much discomfort.

Aerobic activity, like climbing stairs, walking, bicycling or swimming, causes the heart to work harder. Since the heart is a muscle, exercise makes it stronger.

Pick a regular time of day for exercise. For many people, the start of the day is most convenient. Ideally, you should exercise for thirty minutes a day, but ten minutes of activity a day is a good starting place for beginners. Just keep at it. Soon you will have no trouble exercising at least three times a week. And you will enjoy it.

> *Ideally, you should exercise for thirty minutes a day, but ten minutes of activity a day is a good starting place for beginners. Just keep at it.*

As I've said, exercise helps the mind as well as the body. It does so by generating chemicals called "endorphins" that make you feel good and in control. By setting and achieving goals to exercise a bit more over time you get a sense of accomplishment. That accomplishment spills over to other areas. You'll begin to think of yourself as someone who gets things done, by coming at them with patience and determination.

Now you can start keeping a log of your exercise itself. This log, instead of analyzing the sources and patterns of your stress, will record your good fight to cope with those patterns. (For an excellent guide to exercise, see *Weight Loss for African American Women,* by George Edmond Smith.[21])

Labyrinth Walk

Recently, Reverend Dr. Lauren Artress of Grace Cathedral, in San Francisco, helped rekindle interest in walking meditations with his Labyrinth Project. Labyrinths are maze-like circular paths that have one way in and one way out, and are either painted on canvas or built into a floor or the ground. Years ago, people who were unable to journey to Jerusalem used labyrinths as a kind of symbol of that journey. When you walk in a labyrinth, your mind becomes quiet and your soul opens. If there is a labyrinth in your area, you may want to explore it as a walking meditation.

Tonya Moves On....

With ongoing psychotherapy, Tonya was able to address the debilitating depression she was experiencing over the loss of her mother. She recognized the tremendous guilt and feelings of abandonment she experienced each year on Mother's Day and developed a plan for managing these anniversary feelings so she would not be tempted to kill herself. She agreed to consistently follow the prescribed medication regimen. She increased her therapy sessions for several weeks before and after Mother's Day, and spent the day with a friend. She agreed to call for help before doing anything to harm herself. On Mother's Day, she set aside a period for honoring her mother instead of trying to deny her grief. With time, Tonya was less overwhelmed by her sorrow.

STEPS TO OPTIMUM MENTAL HEALTH

Either you get a handle on your stress, or stress will put a hurting on you. Complete a personalized stress management plan for yourself. Choose what works best for you and be aware of anything that gets in the way of sticking to it.

MORE FOR YOUR HEALTH
Book

Gandy, Debrena Jackson: *Sacred Pampering Principles: An African-American Woman's Guide to Self-Care and Inner Renewal.* New York: William Morrow and Company, Inc., 1997.

Movies

What's Love Got to Do With It. Tina Turner uses her spirituality to move toward a better life.

Lady Sings the Blues. Substance abuse is used as a coping device, with fatal consequences.

Chapter Six

Anticipate the Good so that You May Enjoy It

The Path to Recovery and Healthy Self-Esteem

Valerie

As far back as Valerie could remember, she had been ridiculed by friends and family for being thin and light skinned. She had often tried, unsuccessfully, to gain weight, and she wore makeup darker than her true complexion in an attempt to be more like the people who mocked her.

Valerie's few friends told her how lucky she was to not have to worry about her weight, but that didn't fill the void she felt inside. She was so ashamed of herself. She could easily recount the private horror stories about the taunts. At the same time, she went to great lengths to please her friends so they wouldn't leave her.

After a few therapy sessions, Valerie asked her parents to attend one of her appointments with me. They validated her stories about how people had treated her badly. Neither parent understood why Valerie was lighter skinned than they were.

They admitted they had done little to protect her from being teased.

BLACK WOMEN AND SELF-ESTEEM

Healthy self-esteem is about looking at yourself positively. When you look in the mirror, you're proud of the woman you see. She's not perfect and there's work to be done, but her potential is limitless and her eyes are on the prize. She takes pleasure in what she's accomplished, she enjoys the good days and knows how to get through the bad ones, and she looks forward to the future with a sense of confidence and adventure.

Many of us Black American women need to get over some hurdles before we can see that woman in the mirror. But only when we *can* see her and celebrate her can we make better choices for ourselves and the people we love.

The roots of our self-esteem stretch back to those who initially cared for us. When we were children our caregivers were responsible for supplying us with food, clothing, and a safe environment. But they were also obligated to support and nurture our need for acceptance and affirmation, so that we could grow up feeling loved and accepted. Caregivers who themselves struggle with poor self-esteem are unlikely to transmit a sense of positive self-regard to their children.

If we grew up in repressive households where we didn't learn healthy ways to express our anger, our assertiveness, and our sexuality because our parents hadn't worked these issues out for themselves, we are more likely to become adults who still have trouble with these emotions. Too often, the struggle results in a warped sense of ourselves and low self-esteem. It may also mean that we parent no better than we were parented.

Finally, poor or low self-esteem often means that we don't make good personal choices because we don't believe we are worth it. Deciding to have an annual Pap smear and mammogram requires healthy self-esteem. Insisting our partners use condoms means we care about ourselves and our partners. Sticking to a diet or exercise program only happens when we can commit to leaving self-neglect in our past. As Julia Boyd says *In the Company of My Sisters: Black Women and Self-Esteem*: "As adults, our power lies in our ability to have a healthy sense of self-esteem. Self-esteem is power."[22]

The quality of our self-esteem influences the way we develop, move out into the world, and start exploring. As children get older, they want to influence the world around them. They begin to express needs and desires. They also encounter frustrations and develop means of addressing them.

Women in our culture often learn early that to assert themselves is to be stigmatized as wanting to dominate men. If you visit McDonald's and order a Happy Meal, the counter person often asks if you want a boy's or a girl's toy. The boy's toy might be a car, Lego, or action figure; the girl's is frequently a doll. Such experiences teach women, early in life, that it is best to be caretakers and to keep assertiveness and aggression buried.

One theory suggests that women are twice as likely as men to suffer from depression because they are trained to stifle their aggression or direct it inward against themselves. Meanwhile, the boys get cars they can race, or action figures with which they can save the world from bad guys.

For women, that stifled aggression, the emotion we keep chained, frequently demonstrates its power through a critical voice inside that is also a voice of self-hatred. Imagine a judge sitting on her bench in a basement courtroom of your mind. The judge has something insulting to say about everything you do. While shopping you try on a blouse, and the judge says, "You need a larger size. You have a flat butt. That color looks awful on you. Why are you trying to look younger? Everybody sees those ugly wrinkles."

The end result is that we develop a certain amount of sadness or unease, and aren't even aware of what caused it. We may be so upset that we have to find the nearest ice cream store to make us feel better. Eating ice cream when we are trying to make healthier choices is one way the aggression expresses itself outside of our conscious awareness. We punish ourselves by overeating, while we tell ourselves we are enjoying the meal. That ice cream tastes good going down, but the act itself—the ice cream *itself* (especially if you're on a diet)—is not benefiting you.

Our self-esteem isn't helped by the constant bombardment of images with which Black American women can't identify.

Our self-esteem isn't helped by the constant bombardment of images with which Black American women can't identify. True, the advertising and entertainment industry, as well as the internet, have realized that it is in their best interest to recognize Black Americans and our culture. But they continue to create images incompatible with the people we truly are. The NAACP reminded us of this in 1999, when they threatened a boycott of the major networks because of a disgraceful lack of diversity behind and in front of the camera. But often the images of Black people on television continue to be degrading.

As women, we need to be aware of the lack of positive images about ourselves and deliberately work to provide them for our children. Do what you can to let them know of the existence of Black doctors, business owners, lawyers, and writers. Don't let sports and entertainment figures be the only role models for our children.

As women, we need to be aware of the lack of positive images about ourselves and deliberately work to provide them for our children. Do what you can to let them know of the existence of Black doctors, business owners, lawyers, and writers. Don't let sports and entertainment figures be the only role models for our children.

Ask your children to talk about their reaction to negative images from the media. Letting them understand that it is one specific individual who has displayed unacceptable behavior will help them correct any potential negative thoughts or feelings they may develop about being Black.

I can't help but wonder if the results of that classic study conducted in 1940 by Drs. Kenneth B. Clark and his wife, Mamie, both psychologists, would be applicable today. In the study, the Clarks gave Black American children a choice between black and white dolls. The children overwhelmingly chose the white ones. We know the same results were found in 1985, when psychologists Derek Hopson and his wife, Darlene Powell-Hopson, replicated the Clark study. It's frightening to think what the results would be in 2002.

Fortunately, Black Americans have become more aware of themselves as a race. We are choosing art made by us and for us, and are being selective in what we watch. We have learned to purchase products that were advertised with us in mind and that present affirming images. If your daughter likes to play with dolls, make sure many of them look like her. The books you read with her should include those with images of children in worlds similar to hers. By all means, let her read about the variety of human experience, but be sure that among the books she reads are stories that show how girls of color can enjoy a host of experiences, overcome challenges, and display an array of emotions.

> *Be sure that among the books she reads are stories that show how girls of color can enjoy a host of experiences, overcome challenges, and display an array of emotions.*

SEXUALITY

Yes, we struggle with self-image. Even harder, we struggle with our sexuality. Let's face it, many of our parents had only three words to share on the subject of sex: "Don't do it!" American culture, as a whole, has been heavy on prohibitions and the theory that "Silence is Golden." This mindset cost Dr. Jocelyn Elders her job as Surgeon General. She advocated that young people should consider masturbation as an acceptable alternative to casual sex.

Our parents might have signed the permission slips for us to participate in health classes on sexuality, but they frequently avoided talking to us about healthy and responsible sex. Often, what we didn't hear them say was just as important as what they did say.

The messages that we did receive about sex often taught us to be passive. Sex is something that happens to us, as opposed to something we can take responsibility for. Some people believe that this passivity may play a part in unplanned pregnancies. Being unable to take responsibility for our sexuality may inhibit us from using birth control and protecting ourselves from sexually transmitted diseases.

On the other hand, taking responsibility for our sexual actions can lead us to do those things we should do to keep ourselves healthy and to make such basic decisions as to whether to have a baby.

A significant number of Black American women have experienced unwanted sexual activity. These experiences compound any other conflicts about our sexuality and may be associated with inhibited desire, arousal, orgasms, and post-traumatic symptoms. Dr. Gail Elizabeth Wyatt, a noted Black American researcher and author of *Stolen Women: Reclaiming Our Sexuality, Taking Back Our Lives* has extensively studied sexual abuse and consensual sex.[23] Wyatt says that because Black American women are stereotypically perceived as being oversexed, they are reluctant to report sexual abuse because that would serve to reinforce the stereotype. The abuse, and keeping it a secret, have long-term consequences. We as Black

American women are just now giving ourselves permission to talk about the trauma of physical and emotional abuse and its long-term effects. (There's more on this subject in Chapter Eight.)

We must start to develop healthy sexual attitudes in our children. As they discover themselves, we need to provide the right information that helps them appreciate what they're learning. When you listen and respond to their questions in a positive manner, appropriate to their age, you're also implicitly telling them that sexuality is a normal part of life. If your children are found masturbating, address the situation without shaming them for experiencing pleasure. To tell them myths such as that they will go blind or won't have children when they grow up, is to perpetuate false, negative messages. At the same time though, let them know emphatically that no one else should touch their genitals, and if someone does, you need to know about it right away.

> *When you listen and respond to their questions in a positive manner, appropriate to their age, you're also implicitly telling them that sexuality is a normal part of life.*

DEPENDENCY AND SELF-RELIANCE

Dependency is another area of concern to Black American women who are struggling with their self-esteem. Many of us can't accept our own need for care and support because our upbringing has emphasized self-reliance. In *Getting Good Loving: How Black Men and Women Can Make Love Work*, Audrey

B. Chapman says that "Black women get socialized against dependency on Black American men. The 'raising of our daughters and loving of our sons' has created difficulty in our relationships."[24] That is, while mothers are raising daughters to be independent, they're pampering and catering to their sons.

I've spoken earlier about the trouble we can get into when we try to be Superwoman. But I've also emphasized that we must be able to assert ourselves in relationships when we need to. Men who have been raised by doting mothers may not be able to do this. And a Black woman, in turn, may be uneasy about men who want to do things for her and take care of her. Situations like these lead some Black American men to complain about "hard-as-nails" sisters they can't deal with anymore.

What we must try for here is a kind of moderation. We need to be comfortable with being self-reliant when it is necessary, and interdependent when the situation calls for it. Our families and communities work best when we are able to draw upon the strengths and gifts of all members, but also understand and respect the areas where we need help or assistance.

Some Black women grow up with a kind of pseudo-independence that can get them in trouble. How it starts is this. Little Jasmine is learning how to roller blade when she falls and skins her knee. She dashes to her mother looking for solace, but all she gets is, "What are you crying for? I'll give you something to cry about." It's a failure of empathy on the mother's part, and the child learns to hide her need for comfort. There has been a mismatch between what her mother was able to provide and what she desired.

Out of such conflicts between what one needs and what one gets, Jasmine learns a pseudo-independence. That is, she no longer seeks to satisfy her own needs but takes on the role of caring for everyone else in the hope that she will, in some way, get these hidden needs met. Or Jasmine may follow a different course, and grow up spending time and energy trying to get others to take care of her. In this scenario, Jasmine neglects herself in the hope that others will notice this and provide the care and affection she desperately needs.

As children, when we are dependent on others for our care, we are leery about holding them directly responsible for our disappointments and frustrations. It's hard to get angry with our parents. If we express our anger or displeasure, we fear they may leave us or punish us in some way. But just because we can't express it effectively doesn't mean it goes away. Instead we turn this anger or displeasure against ourselves. We think we are bad or that we don't know how to act and never will know. This process, which happens outside of our conscious awareness, leaves us with negative feelings about ourselves.

Although we live in a politically correct climate, we still have to deal with the negative stereotypes too many Americans have about Black people. When many of us attended elementary school, historical references about African-Americans primarily pertained to slavery. There was little information to help define ourselves positively. We were fortunate if we had family members, churches, and/or friends who represented or steered us toward alternative, affirming, and more positive resources by showing us the considerable positive side of African American experience.

Alex Haley's *Roots: The Saga of an American Family* (Doubleday. New York. 1976) and other literary works reminded us that we had a rich past about which we knew little because of an oppressive society that found it in its best interest to ignore it.[25] This lack of information left many of us misinformed, and some of us rejected our past. Some Black Americans still do not want to have anything to do with Kwanzaa or other activities that connect us to our African origins. Yet for us as a people, just as for us as individuals, by coming to terms with our past, we learn to affirm it.

Valerie Moves On...

Valerie suffered such low self-esteem that when she wasn't sabotaging potential relationships out of fear of rejection she was desperately clinging to those few friends she had. Much of her hostility and aggression were directed toward herself. She secretly binged on food, hoping to gain weight and had considered buying some illegal steroids to bulk up. She found therapy painful and cut it off prematurely. Obviously, she chose a poor way to deal with low self-esteem.

STEPS TO OPTIMUM MENTAL HEALTH

Continue to acquaint yourself with the Judge within and decrease her power to keep you from feeling positive about yourself. Also try to notice whether you have set unrealistic expectations for yourself. How do you feel when you don't accomplish them?

An Exercise

The first step towards healthier self-regard and self esteem is to identify the Judge's voice within. For the next week, you need to commit to listening to what the Judge is saying, and gauging the devastation she renders in your life. Follow these steps:

In your journal, keep track of the major discontents you experience.

· What makes you sad, annoyed or disturbed?
· When did these feelings begin? Was there a certain event that triggered them?
· What thoughts ran through your mind when this happened? Were they critical or affirming? Do you now have second thoughts?
· Are there disparaging remarks you regularly make about yourself?

After a week or two of this exercise you should begin to be acquainted with the Judge sitting on your bench. Your journal will be your primary tool, but you may also want to ask a close friend if she notices that you are being critical of yourself, and if so how.

Now it is time to decrease the Judge's authority. You must begin to challenge her declarations. If the Judge says, "You are hopeless. You are a failure," or other critical statements, you need to counterattack with less judgmental, more realistic, statements like, "I wasn't as successful

continued on next page

continued from previous page

as I wanted to be with this project. There were some aspects of it that I was not aware of and therefore could not plan for. Now that I've been through this once, I'll be better able to do a stronger job next time."

This needs to be an ongoing exercise. The Judge has a lot of power, but you can make a significant dent in her ability to direct hostility and aggression toward you just by identifying her presence.

MORE FOR YOUR HEALTH

Books

Stolen Women: Reclaiming Our Sexuality, Taking Back Our Lives, Gail Elizabeth Wyatt. New York: John Wiley & Sons, Inc., 1997

In the Company of my Sisters: Black Women and Self-Esteem, Julia A. Boyd. New York: Penguin Books, 1993

Movies

Introducing Dorothy Dandridge. Shows how early trauma can affect later relationships and sexual functioning.

Marnie. Early trauma is forgotten but continues to impact on day-to-day functioning.

CHAPTER SEVEN

WHEN SPIDER WEBS UNITE, THEY CAN TIE UP A LION

Negotiating the Mental Health System

Lorraine

For as long as she could remember, she had stood on her own two feet. She despised the idea that at thirty-five she needed help. But law school was more than she had bargained for. There were only two Black Americans in her class and they barely spoke to each other. She felt so isolated. On top of that, now she had to argue cases in front of others. She was losing it. She'd get panic attacks the night before a major presentation. Her heart raced, she sweated uncontrollably, and a lump appeared in her throat. Soon, she was having dizzy spells. Her doctor had prescribed medication, but wouldn't give her a refill until she talked with someone.

"I'm not crazy, but I soon will be," she said when we first met.

PRIMARY, SECONDARY, AND TERTIARY INTERVENTION

Nothing is saner than to seek help for our mental health needs, but our track record indicates we believe otherwise. Part of the problem, of course, isn't of our making. The U.S. Surgeon General's supplemental report, *Mental Health: Culture, Race, and Ethnicity* points out that limited insurance coverage and lack of quality providers are some of the barriers Black Americans face in accessing the mental healthcare system.

But while we can't, suddenly, change this harsh reality, we can change our attitude. Once people decide that it is o.k. to seek help, they can usually find what they need. So the first step is to drop our stereotypes about mental health, acknowledge that we are not functioning at our best, and understand that we don't have to wait so long before reaching out. As you would have preventive maintenance performed on your car to keep it from breaking down unexpectedly, so should you perform preventive maintenance on the parts of your self in order to maintain and improve good mental health.

Primary intervention is what providers call the first stage of care. This is preventive maintenance, where trouble gets nipped in the bud by teaching meditation, conflict resolution skills and other exercises that keep the engine running smoothly. Conflict resolution skills go a long way toward improving relationships and building a sense of community.

Secondary intervention is the early diagnosis and treatment of depression. The goal is to prevent the disease from disabling the patient.

Tertiary intervention focuses on those living with, say, schizophrenia, and who have a record of multiple hospitalizations and recurrences. The goal here is to stabilize the person with medications to prevent further deterioration. It is unlikely that we'll ever have a world without mental or physical illnesses, but we can create an environment where prevention is more a part of our mental health strategy.

I said that we need to change our attitude. Here's a new one you can consider. While walking life's tightrope, we're balancing, on one hand, challenges, disappointments, and pain; on the other are our inner determination, tenacity and drive to confront life head-on. When the scales begin to tip more toward the stressors, it is time to look for the net below. As with any disease, the longer we wait to get help, the higher the risk of unwanted consequences. Suicide, disability and long-term impairment are some of the results of untreated depression.

> *The longer we wait to get help, the higher the risk of unwanted consequences.*

FINDING CARE

What is it like to participate in mental health treatment? Before I explain, it is important to know that primary care physicians prescribe the majority of mental health medications. Because stigma and other issues prevent many from contacting a psychiatrist, health officials have increased their efforts to provide primary care physicians with the tools necessary to understand and treat mental health disorders. So start with your primary care doctor and she will let you know if a specialized provider is needed.

If your primary care doctor recommends that you see a mental health provider, your first appointment with that specialist will involve an evaluation. Whether you are seeing her privately or in a clinic, the psychotherapist or psychiatrist's goal is to gather information about your current concerns and take a mental health history.

While the primary care physician is where many people start to seek help, if you don't have a primary care doctor you are not cut off. Each state receives federal dollars earmarked for mental health services for those on Medicaid or whose income is below a certain level.

These funds are usually managed by the Commissioner of Mental Health for your state. Contact the Department of Health in your state. They should be able to direct you to local mental health agencies. They may also have funds available to allow you to see a primary care doctor and get necessary medications.

Mental health professionals ideally want to establish a helping relationship with their patients. Professionalism generally requires that we divulge very little personal information about ourselves, because we want our patients to focus on themselves, not us. Your sessions with the practitioner are about you. Some of us may not shake your hand when we first greet you, but please don't take that the wrong way. The patient, for a number of reasons, may have real issues about being touched.

After you've given the standard information—name, age, marital status, etc.—the therapist is likely to ask you open-ended questions about:

- the reason you are seeking consultation
- the length of time the difficulties have been present
- what you believe triggered the current difficulties
- whether these problems occurred before, and what helped then
- whether you've had other mental health difficulties
- your history of emergency room visits or hospitalizations
- what medications and natural supplements you take
- any difficulties connected with your menstrual cycle, use of birth control devices, menopause
- specific symptoms, such as changes in your sleep pattern or appetite? crying spells?
- suicidal or homicidal thoughts, past or present
- attempts to harm yourself
- whether you use alcohol or drugs in such a way as to have a negative impact on your health, work and/or relationships
- major causes of stress in your life—such as deaths, divorce, abortions, sexual or physical assault, emotional or sexual abuse in childhood
- symptoms that suggest you are having difficulty distinguishing reality versus unreality—for example, hallucinations (seeing things others can't see), hearing voices, smelling unusual odors.
- how you interpret a proverb. For example, what is the meaning of "*One monkey don't stop no show?*"

The therapist may also ask you to give the date, time, and place, and ask you to do simple calculations.

Respond to such questions with confidence that the therapist is trying to determine your current difficulties and to gauge your mind's organizational skills. Don't be surprised if there are silences. These may feel a bit awkward but the therapist wants you to take the lead in describing your concerns, what you believe cause them, and how you have tried to address them.

> *Don't be surprised if there are silences.*

At first, you may feel uncomfortable sharing personal information. This is normal. As you work with the therapist and come to know her, you will become more comfortable telling her your most private thoughts. As in all doctor-patient relationships, what you say doesn't leave the office.

You may have noticed that I used the term *working with* the therapist or psychiatrist. Mental health treatment is not generally something that is done *to* you. It works best when you are an active participant. It's your life and your happiness that are at stake here. So a good way to start a session is simply to say what comes to your mind. The therapist can then take her cue from what *you* have to say about your problems and solutions.

> *Mental health treatment works best when you are an active participant.*

Sometimes we are reluctant to voice our thoughts for fear the therapist will label us as crazy and have us hospitalized. But it is important to reveal these difficult thoughts because they help the mental health professional make an accurate diagnosis and develop the best treatment plan for you. If you are experiencing frightening events that make you fear you are losing your mind, the therapist needs to hear this from you.

AGAINST THEIR WILL

All states have laws regulating involuntary commitments, which means hospitalizing a person without her consent. Years ago, it was easier to have someone committed, and the process was therefore abused. Today, tougher laws protect us all.

But if you have a family member with a mental illness and the relative is putting you or herself at risk, you *must* take these statements seriously and take necessary action. That means getting this person to a mental health professional who can evaluate her condition. If the person is cooperative, go with her to the nearest emergency room. Your community may have a crisis team that will come to your house to give help. (It's helpful to check out such resources in advance, but you can also find them at the last minute through the operator.)

If the person is *not* cooperative, you have two options. You can call the police for help in getting the person to the emergency room. If the police won't respond without a court order, you may go to the local hall of justice and ask a judge to issue an emergency petition. You will have to tell the judge about your relative's behavior and, if applicable, explain her history of illness. After the judge issues an emergency petition, the police will have the authority to take your sick relative to the emergency room, to undergo an evaluation by mental health care professionals.

If at any time the situation gets out of control, use your common sense. While most people who are suffering mental illness aren't dangerous, you must protect yourself from harm.

After an evaluation, involuntary commitment requires recommendations from two mental health professionals or a judge. There are specific criteria that must be documented. You must have a mental health diagnosis and you must be a danger to yourself or others. If you are evaluated and the recommendation for hospitalization is made, it is because the mental health professionals do not believe you are safe at home. It is difficult to hear the recommendation and some might protest, "I'll be alright." The professional wants to protect you from impulsive acts that can lead to permanent damage. Your best course is to look at it positively. By agreeing to your hospitalization, you are saying to yourself and to others that you want to take an active part in your recovery.

CHOOSING HELP

Many African-American women want to see African-American female therapists. But only two percent of all psychiatrists in the country are Black, and fewer still are female, so the chances are slim that you'll get one. That's no excuse to abandon your search. If you can't find a Black American female psychiatrist, you'll just have to be more aware of what the therapist—of whatever race—can do for you. Give the doctor a chance; do not judge ability just by the color of the doctor's skin.

Although Dr. Smith may be white, does she have what it takes to empathize with your African-American story? Can she appreciate the impact that racial issues play in your distress? Does this doctor really care about you? Do you feel comfortable with her and do you believe that she will help you? Trust is an important consideration.

If you do visit a psychiatrist who is not a Black American, for your own comfort and peace of mind you might want to put the following on the table:

- Explain to the therapist that racial issues are important to you.
- Ask the therapist about her experiences with Black American patients.
- Be willing to explain customs or terms that the therapist might not understand. Not everyone knows what a straightening comb is, for example.
- Be willing to address concerns as they come up. For instance, if a therapist addresses you by your first name and you are uncomfortable with this, tell her and explain the history associated with undue familiarity, and the disrespect Black Americans associate with not being addressed as Mr. or Mrs.

It is quite appropriate for you to size up the therapist during your initial consultation. You may want to learn about her training, her general treatment style, her fees, and what she will charge for missed appointments.

While racial, cultural, and sexual differences are important factors in choosing a therapist, you first and foremost need a competent and caring mental health professional. Clinicians who are disrespectful, or who violate boundaries (unwanted touching, or seductive comments or behaviors) are not common but do exist. If you are unable to establish a trusting relationship with a therapist and have explored the reasons why, consider interviewing others. Therapy requires trust and commitment on your part. But have an open mind and be objective.

SURVEY SAYS!

In preparing for a presentation to the American Psychiatric Association, I surveyed about twenty-five African American clinicians in the Baltimore-Washington, D.C. area. I wanted to find out what their own treatment experiences were like and how they treated African-American females. I wanted to know what methods of treatment they found most effective. The ultimate aim was to educate non-African-Americans about what worked when treating Black women.

The clinicians I surveyed ranged in age from thirty to seventy years of age. They held advanced degrees and they each had between ten to forty years of clinical experience treating African-American women. Their treatment procedures ran the course from behavioral to pastoral counseling to psychoanalysis. Seventy-five percent reported being in treatment themselves— either one-on-one, in a group, or in marriage counseling.

The majority of these clinicians had been in therapy with a therapist of a different racial background. They reported that, especially at the beginning of the treatment, they felt mistrustful of the therapist. Several mentioned working with Jewish female therapists, whom they felt were able to relate to them because of shared experiences with injustices. They reported how important it was to talk openly about racial differences. All reported their therapy was helpful.

The clinicians surveyed worked well with therapists who knew about and understood Black American experiences and culture, and who had Black American colleagues. Several felt they had to spend significant time educating their therapists about cultural issues, but this decreased over the course of treatment. One reported she should have been paid for the time she spent schooling her therapist. The conclusion here is to be direct, honest, and open with your therapist. Be slow to judge, and give her—no matter what color her skin—a chance to help you.

Psychopharmacology

Psychopharmacology, the branch of pharmacology that deals with the study of psychoactive drugs, contributes greatly to the treatment of mental disorders. It includes many new, more effective medications that have replaced older ones. The new medications are based on the premise that most mental conditions are caused by an imbalance in certain brain chemicals, like dopamine, serotonin and norepinephrine. These chemicals, or neurotransmitters, facilitate communication among the brain cells. The new drugs treat mental disorders by returning the chemicals to a normal balanced level. The medications are classified broadly by the disorders they treat.

GETTING USED TO YOUR MEDICATION

The wide variety of medication offers many options for treating depression. Some of the medications are used in combination with others. Most of them take at least two weeks before significant improvement is seen in the symptoms. Unless there are serious side effects, most doctors want you to stay on the medication for at least six weeks to see if it is effective. If you have side effects tell your doctor, but don't stop taking the drugs unless under the doctor's direction.

In considering what medication to prescribe, your doctor

will usually take into account what specific symptoms you are experiencing with your depression. If you are having anxious feelings, a medication with an antianxiety effect might be the first choice. If you are overweight and overeating, your doctor might prescribe one less likely to cause weight gain. Most patients notice that the physical symptoms of their depression improve before their mood does.

> *Most patients notice that the physical symptoms of their depression improve before their mood does.*

Your doctor or pharmacist will share information with you on the most common side effects of particular drugs. Changes in sexual desire or functioning are side effects that can be especially distressing to some patients. Some don't like to talk about such topics with their doctor, but I strongly recommend that you speak up. Sometimes changes in the dosage or the type of medication you're taking can help you, but your doctor won't know to do this unless you tell her.

Once the symptoms of your depression are under control, you will need to remain on the medicine for several months. If you've had depression before, you may need to remain on the medicine for up to a year or even longer. Of course, your own doctor will have the final say on the length of your medical treatment.

Here are some issues you and your doctor should discuss before she gives you a drug or before you stop taking your medication:

- the kind and dosage of all the drugs and natural supplements you are using.
- when to stop taking medication. If stopped abruptly some may have uncomfortable side effects.
- how much alcohol, *if any,* you may have during treatment.
- what other kinds and what dosages of medication your family physician is prescribing.

If you're anxious about using drugs, ask the doctor if you can start with a lower dose and increase it slowly. Among the major drugs available are:

ANTIDEPRESSANTS

Antidepressants are divided into older and newer drugs.

Older Medications

Brand	Chemical Name
Anafranil™	clomipramine
Ascendin™	amoxapine
Elavil™	amitriptyline
Ludiomil™	maprotiline
Norpramin™	desipramine
Pamelor™	nortriptyline
Sinequan™	doxepin
Surmontil™	trimipramine
Tofranil™	imipramine
Vivactil™	protriptyline

These older medications may have more potential for side effects that particularly impact the cardiovascular system. Despite this, they are effective antidepressant medications.

The latest new drugs carry less risk of serious side effects.

New Medications

Brand	Chemical Name
Celexa™	citalopram
Desyrel™	trazodone)
Effexor™	venlafaxine
Luvox™	fluvoxamine
Paxil™	paroxetine
Prozac™	fluoxetine
Prozac Weekly™	fluoxetine HCl
Remeron™	mirtazapine
Serzone™	nefazodone
Wellbutrin™	bupropion
Zoloft™	sertraline

Another older class of drugs that targets a different chemical system is often used when the depression shows symptoms of increased appetite and increased sleep or fatigue. With these older medications it is necessary to follow a special diet and avoid using certain other medications to prevent potential side effects to the cardiovascular system.

These drugs are:

Parnate™	tranylcypromine
Nardil™	phenelzine

There are other drugs that treat both the emotional and physical problems associated with depression.

ANTIPSYCHOTICS (MAJOR TRANQUILIZERS)

Many of us have heard of Thorazine™ (chlorpromazine). It is one of the early medications that was used to treat psychosis. The illnesses that antipsychotic medications treat range from schizophrenia, to bipolar disorder, to dementia and delirium. The Thorazine family of drugs can be divided into two categories: atypical and phenothiazines. The atypical drugs are those most recently developed and some are believed to have fewer serious side effects than the earlier phenothiazine medications.

Atypical Drugs

Clozaril™	clozapine
Geodon™	ziprasidone
Haldol™	haloperidol
Loxitane™	loxapine
Moban™	molindone
Navane™	thiothixene
Orap™	pimozide
Risperdal™	risperidone
Seroquel™	quetiapine
Zyprexa™	olanzapine

Phenothiazine Drugs

Compazine™	prochlorperazine
Etrafon™	perphenazine/amitriptyline
Serentil™	mesoridazine besylate

Stelazine™	trifluoperazine
Thioridazine™	thioridazine hcl
Trilafon™	perphenazine

Your doctor may use these medications and others to treat specific symptoms such as severe agitation, hallucinations and paranoia. Depending on the symptoms and diagnosis, these medications may be used briefly or for a long-term. Researchers have found some Black Americans metabolize these medicines slower and may require lower doses, so ask your doctor whether you should begin by taking lower doses of these drugs.

ANTI-ANXIETY MEDICATIONS (MINOR TRANQUILIZERS)

This group of medications targets anxiety disorders, like panic and generalized anxiety disorder. These new drugs have less sedative side effects. Some of them may be addictive, which has sometimes led to their abuse.

Benzodiazepines

Ativan™	lorazepam
Librium™	chlordiazepoxide
Limbitrol™	chlordiazepexoide/ amitriptyline
Tranxene™	chlorazepate dipotassium
Valium™	diazepam
Xanax™	alprazolam

Other Antianxiety Medicines

Atarax™	hydroxyzine
Buspar ™	buspirone
Effexor™	venlafaxine
Miltown™	maprobamate
Paxil™	paroxetine
Sinequan™	doxepin
Vistaril™	hydroxyzine pamoate

The following medications are usually used to control panic disorders:

Klonopin™	clonazepam
Xanax™	alprazolam
Zoloft™	sertraline

Anti-anxiety medications may be used briefly or for a long term. The tendencies of some of these drugs to depress brain activity make it important that patients strictly follow the prescribed directions. After the doctor says she's going to write a prescription, discuss the issues and, in addition, ask your doctor specifically about the drug's side effects or potential addictive qualities.

ANTI-MANIC MEDICATIONS/MOOD STABILIZERS

Lithium and Depakote™ are the most frequently prescribed medications to regulate mood. Researchers are using several other anticonvulsant medications to target manic symptoms. When you use these medications, your blood will have to be monitored to assure you are receiving the correct safe and therapeutic dose.

ALTERNATIVE/NATURAL TREATMENTS

There has been a lot of media coverage about natural substances such as St. John's Wort, which some claim can treat depression, and about other natural supplements that claim to treat other emotional disorders. I, like most of my colleagues, won't publicly endorse any of these products until they have been proven effective.

> *If you're taking an herbal supplement, be sure to let your doctor know. She'll want to find out whether the remedies have been helping you or not.*

The Food and Drug Administration does not regulate these products, so no standards have been set for the quality and quantity of the active ingredients in these compounds. Most importantly, the jury is still out on how effective any of them really are. If you're taking an herbal supplement, be sure to let your doctor know. She'll want to find out whether the remedies have been helping you or not.

TREATMENTS WITH AND WITHOUT DRUGS

Although sometimes drug treatment is recommended in addition to therapy, various treatments for mental illness are available that don't require drugs. While medications may help control the symptoms of an illness, therapy can help you discover and use more effective coping skills. National organizations such as the American Psychiatric Association have developed Practice Guidelines for non-drug treatments that have been shown to have positive results:

Light Therapy

Seasonal Affective Disorder is believed to be caused by changes in brain chemicals due to decreased exposure to light during the fall and winter months. Light therapy involves daily treatment with specialized lamps to counterbalance these suspected changes.

Regular exercise is good for depressive disorders. It releases certain brain chemicals that combat depressive symptoms. A regular exercise program can complement other treatments.

Exercise

Regular exercise is good for depressive disorders. It releases certain brain chemicals that combat depressive symptoms. A regular exercise program can complement other treatments.

Psychotherapy

There are various forms of psychotherapy, otherwise known as talk therapy. This treatment is about voicing your thoughts and secrets. From these, the therapist can begin to understand the root of the problem that brought you to therapy.

Cognitive Behavioral

This treatment focuses on the thoughts an individual has that contribute to her emotional response to particular kinds of stress. Once these thoughts are recognized and understood, the patient can start learning to cope with the stress. Treatment is often brief and targets specific symptoms.

Psychodynamic

This treatment is based on the theory that thoughts, feelings, and impulses outside of awareness contribute to current feelings and behaviors. Sessions are usually once or twice a week for an extended period.

Psychoanalysis

Here treatment focuses on conflicts outside of awareness that lead to symptoms and inhibitions. The psychoanalyst is interested in the workings of your mind and how conflicts may contribute to your difficulties. Sessions are usually four to five times a week, and the use of a reclining couch is recommended. Treatment usually lasts several years.

Supportive Therapy

The focus here is on helping the patient handle external sources of stress. The therapist is usually more active and may give directions or advice. The treatment helps to strengthen existing coping styles.

Family Therapy

This treatment involves two or more relatives. It focuses on family dynamics and how they contribute to difficulties in the family unit. Members may also see a therapist individually.

Marital Therapy

This treatment is for couples who are seeking to improve the quality of their relationship. A spouse may also see another therapist.

Group Therapy

This treatment involves several people who may have specific difficulties in common, like controlling anger, or the patients in the group may be people who can benefit from group interaction to address specific issues. One or more therapists may lead the group. The group may operate within a defined time frame, or members may come and go as their specific difficulties are addressed.

Self-Help Therapy

People with similar concerns meet to give mutual support and share what they have learned. Alcoholics Anonymous is an example of such a group. Leadership is shared, usually by people who are experts on a particular difficulty.

Psychiatric Rehabilitation

This treatment helps people address the consequences that severe psychiatric disability has had on their functioning. Psychiatric rehabilitation helps patients succeed at work and enhances their social skills.

Lorraine Moves On....

Medication brought Lorraine's anxiety under control. Therapy helped her identify the conflicts she had about expressing anger and being assertive. She struggled with a long-standing desire to please other people and avoid making waves. She was unwilling to participate in extended therapy, so her concerns were only partially addressed. She decided to practice real estate law to avoid the stressful confrontations that came with being in the courtroom. A greater commitment to therapy would have helped her expand her choices.

> *Learn about mental health treatment options before a crisis, and before you reach your last nerve.*

STEPS TO OPTIMUM MENTAL HEALTH

Learn about mental health treatment options before a crisis, and before you reach your last nerve. Continue to use your personal stress management plan, and consider getting help if you think you need it.

MORE FOR YOUR HEALTH

Books

Phillips, Crystal: *The Me I Knew I Could Be*. New York: St Martin's Press, 2001. Personal account of weight loss and seeking therapy

Yalom, Irwin D.: *Love's Executioner and Other Tales of Psychotherapy*. New York:

Basic Books, Inc., 1989. Case histories of patients in therapy for common problems.

Movie

Good Will Hunting. A somewhat dramatized therapy experience is chronicled.

Chapter Eight
A Single Bracelet
Does Not Jingle

Love, Intimacy, and Relationships

Aleshya

Aleshya celebrated her forty-third birthday alone. No lover, no friends, no children. All of her energy and love went into her job, with nothing left for other people, so when the big day came, there was no one to sing "Happy Birthday."

The source of Aleshya's loneliness went back to her childhood when her younger brother was born with sickle cell disease. Any nurturing her mother had provided before her brother's birth disappeared after he was born. To make matters worse, her mother had her own issues, and was too busy satisfying those needs to notice how much her own brother, Alyesha's uncle, enjoyed baby-sitting Aleshya. His hugs and kisses were innocent at first, but what followed was not.

Her uncle told Aleshya that it was their secret. Other people would envy her if they knew, he whispered. At least she was getting some affection, but even that ended when she got her first period. She could get pregnant now, so he stopped. The abuse left her feeling mistrust, pain, and shame. She couldn't allow herself to be close to anyone. When she became an adult, work was much safer than relationships.

LEARNING TO LOVE YOURSELF

What's love got to do with mental health? A whole lot. In fact, in assessing our mental history, what psychoanalysts and other therapists especially want to know about, besides our ability to work, is our ability to give and receive love.

> *What psychoanalysts and other therapists especially want to know about, besides our ability to work, is our ability to give and receive love.*

The desire to be known, loved, and connected to others gets many of us out of bed each day. We require closeness and connection for survival. From birth, we are dependent on the care of another person to develop into adulthood. It is this first relationship that lays the groundwork for our continued desire for closeness throughout life. If our early caretaking went reasonably well, we want to be touched, kissed, and to make love, and will go the extra mile to get these satisfactions. If our early caretaking did not go well, we may not know how to get these satisfactions through our connection to others.

Michael Jackson reminded us in his song, *Man in the Mirror*, that if you want to make the world a better place, start changing things with the man in the mirror. Now it's time for you to ask the woman in the mirror to change her ways. That means getting acquainted with your true self as opposed to the *front* you are always showing to the rest of the folks. It means believing in yourself and learning to love, cherish, and accept yourself .

For many of us, it isn't easy to say, "I love you" to our reflection. We have a Bachelor of Arts degree in self-criticism, a Master's in self-rejection, and we are working on completing a Doctorate in self-destruction. We didn't learn this behavior overnight. We were raised in a culture that requires us to be dissatisfied with ourselves in order to drive the economy. If we accept ourselves for the wonderful creations we are, it would not be necessary to buy that Cadillac Escalade to solicit stares of approval and envy from other people. Many of us were raised by mothers like Alyesha's, who didn't know how to affirm themselves, and so couldn't teach us.

One of the ways we beat ourselves up is by focusing on our failures. Harold S. Kushner writes, in *How Good Do We Have to Be? A New Understanding of Guilt and Forgiveness*, "When we let ourselves be defined in our minds by our worst moment instead of our best ones, we learn to think of ourselves as people who never get it right, rather than as capable people who make an occasional, thoroughly human mistake."[26] Self-love and acceptance includes the ability to cut ourselves a break sometimes. Focusing on the positive leads us toward self-acceptance.

The process of reaching self-love and self-acceptance requires work. Earlier you read about the two forces we have within us: one that fuels our desire to be connected with other people and encourages us to keep the human race alive by reproducing and caring for each other; the other that seeks to preserve or protect us and leads us to be aggressive when necessary, to prevent harm to ourselves or the people we love.

In living out the script that this culture has written for us as women, we haven't had a lot of encouragement to openly express this assertiveness. Most of us are not boxers like Laila Ali and Jacqueline Frazier-Lyde, daughters of Muhammad Ali and Joe Frazier. If we aren't expressing this aggression, and it doesn't disappear, what happens to it? Well, instead of having a boxing match with other people, we start throwing punches at ourselves. Every time we tell ourselves we are unlovable or unacceptable, we are throwing a left hook to our chins. Each criticism adds to the previous blow, and if you do this enough, and become severely depressed, you're like a fighter who's been hit in the jaw too often and becomes punch drunk.

As you did in the judge exercise in Chapter Six, you must again look for clues that show you are using your own self-protective impulses against yourself. Once you've begun to see the ways you beat yourself up, you can begin the job of showing yourself the love and affection you need. Don't just wait for other people to say they love you. If you really desire and deserve some flowers, and other people don't provide them, buy them for yourself and sign the card, "Your Number One Fan and Lover." Given enough nurturing, your inner self will begin to feel affirmed and appreciated.

RELATIONSHIPS

Once you are committed to moving toward greater self-love, and self-respect and acceptance, you can consider entering relationships with other people. Many of us have given up on

An Exercise

A Love Affair with Myself

· Each day say or write something positive about yourself. If you have difficulty getting started, ask your friends and family for examples.

· Each day do something to nurture yourself: take a bath, meditate, exercise, or read *Sacred Pampering Principles: An African-American Woman's Guide to Self-Care and Inner Renewal* by Debrena Jackson Gandy [Self-published; 1998] for more tips.

· Each day review how often you have thrown a punch at yourself. Commit yourself to decreasing these attacks over the long haul.

· Begin to be aware of critical comments other people make about you. If what people say to you isn't helpful, it is negative. Point out, diplomatically, that you don't mind constructive feedback but you aren't willing to be a punching bag.

· If you are in an abusive relationship, consider getting professional help, but get out of it now.

that goal—once burned, twice shy. We are reluctant to let our guard down, because when we were hurt or disappointed the first time, it was devastating. Maybe we were rejected and abandoned, maybe we were over-controlled, engulfed, or outright abused. Such experiences inhibit us from trying new relationships, be they friendships, romances, or even parenting.

You may be in this place: telling yourself that you can't live through another breakup or disappointment. You may feel that way because you were looking to the other person to ful-

> *You may have wanted the relationship to prove that you are acceptable, lovable, and good enough. But these are tasks that you must first be able to do for yourself before you can have a healthy relationship with someone else.*

fill some needs that you really must fill for yourself. You may have wanted the relationship to prove that you are acceptable, lovable, and good enough. But these are tasks that you must first be able to do for yourself before you can have a healthy relationship with someone else.

If you approach your relationships—with your friends, your children, or your partner—with the desire that they complete you, you will be repeatedly disappointed. If you have already experienced your fair share of these disappointments, it is time for a time out and exploration. While self-help books may help some, you will derive more benefit from spending some time in therapy uncovering these self-defeating patterns.

I took lessons in windsurfing and I know all too well that learning the sport involves falling. Being in relationships is also about taking risks and possibly falling. But nobody needs to keep falling forever. This time, you can be better prepared for entering a relationship because this time you will know better just what you are looking for. In fact, there are a variety of potentially healthy relationships. We don't always want the same thing from each one.

In *Necessary Losses,* Judith Viorst breaks down the types of friendships we may have over the course of a lifetime.[28] These friendships include:

> *Being in relationships is also about taking risks and possibly falling. But nobody needs to keep falling forever.*

- *convenience friends,* people whose lives we intersect, such as neighbors, who provide mutual aid but always maintain their public face and don't get too close.
- *special interest friends,* people with whom we share a certain activity, such as an exercise class. We do things together without becoming intimate.
- *historical friends,* with whom we may have little in common anymore but who are an important part of our past.
- *crossroads friends,* who share a crucial time in our lives, such as college. A special intimacy remains even when we haven't seen them for a long time.
- *close friends,* friends with whom we have ongoing relationships in an intimate way. We reveal our inner thoughts, wishes, and fears to our close friends.
- *cross-generational friendships,* which usually demonstrate a special intimacy because they are similar to a mother-daughter relationship.

Some of us have limited experience establishing healthy and mutually rewarding relationships like those Viorst identifies. If we were really fortunate, we witnessed our mothers, aunts, and grandmothers in loving and affirming relationships with other people. If we didn't have those positive role models before, we can start now to explore ways of connecting with other women.

Making friendships with women is essential to our mental health, but we may run into barriers. Sometimes our competitive instincts cause friction among our women friends. If we had older or younger sisters, we were always competing for our parents' love and attention, and we may bring that same tension to our relationships with other women. Or, if we competed with our mothers for our fathers' affections, we may find it hard to turn off this behavior when other women try to be our friends. In this situation, our desire to compete for the prize of a man's attention may get in the way of having cooperative relationships with other women.

It is quite natural to want to have a loving, nurturing relationship with our sister friends. If we were fortunate, we had loving, nurturing relationships with our mothers, and want to experience that again. Still, some of us may be uncomfortable around other women because we may actually be attracted to them and fear we are lesbians.

Yes, it is also true that some of us are sexually attracted to other women and need to be honest with ourselves about it. Letting ourselves be aware of our true feelings allows us more opportunity to make conscious choices instead of being driven by feelings we are trying to deny.

Loving and supportive relationships with other women can be empowering and life-saving. Studies of women with breast cancer showed that women who participated in a support group with other breast cancer survivors lived longer than those who didn't. As Black American women, the church has been a place where we obtained social support. Some of our spiritual leaders believe we can enrich this experience. Reverend Cecilia Williams Bryant, while at Bethel AME Church in Baltimore and throughout her ministry in Africa and the Caribbean, ardently advocated that women should share deeper relationships with each other. In her book, *Kiamsha: A Spiritual Discipline for African-American Women,* [p. 135] she includes the African American SisterCare Code:[29]

- I will not speak negatively of another woman or allow a woman to be spoken of negatively in my presence.
- In confidentiality, I receive that which is shared with me as a Sacred Trust.
- I am not passive when another woman is engaged in self-destructive attitudes or behaviors.
- I do not obstruct the life of another woman, emotionally, professionally, sexually, financially, or spiritually.
- I heighten every woman's sense of beauty by my affirmation of her.
- I do not exploit, ridicule, pervert, perjure, or condescend to the Gift of another woman.
- I daily make intercessions for women in leadership by Name, that their visibility does not create undue suffering.
- What I bring into the Life of another Woman, by the Spirit of God, will be manifested in my Own. (Galatians 6: 7)

While reading about other women does not involve actual physical interaction, therapists also recommend connecting with other women through their literature. We connect whenever we are able to find ourselves in their stories. Fictional and real-life characters in books can provide us with role models.

In learning how others managed life choices, we expand our data banks. Some of us remain entangled in distressing situations because we are unaware of other options, or we believe we are the only ones who have ever endured a specific hardship. By reading, or listening to tapes, we can have a front row seat to view the spirits of our sisters; we can realize that our experiences are normal, and we will feel less isolated. We may then be able to view our experiences in a more positive light.

Books can be therapeutic Many have drawn strength and courage from Maya Angelou's *I Know Why the Caged Bird Sings*,[30] and from Bonnie St. John Deane's *Succeeding Sane: Making Room for Joy in a Crazy World*. Deane tells her own story, that of a United States Olympic skiing medalist and Rhodes Scholar, who had also lost a leg when she was five.[31]

> *"Winners," she writes, "are those who get up and finish."*

Deane, a Black woman, became a member of the US Disabled Ski Team in 1984. Leading after the first run of the slalom race, she and an Austrian woman, who was behind her in time, fell in the second run. Deane explains that the Austrian skier won the gold, and she took the silver because the Austrian got up faster. "Winners," she writes, "are those who get up and finish." Deane's story has much to offer people who need a sense of connection and understanding when facing life's challenges.

Certainly, in entering deep emotional relationships, we need all the courage and support that we can dig up. The search for a partner or soul mate to love and be loved by is fraught with challenges. Both partners bring past experiences, fantasies, and "home training" to the table. You learned lessons about relationships every time you saw your mother prepare a meal for her partner, or decide not to prepare it. You learned whenever you saw them express love and affection for each other, or when they lived lives with repressed hatred and rage. You learned by what they said and did not say, by what they did and did not do. You also learned by the way they responded to your displays of affection to them, and to your questions about love and sexuality. Along the line, you probably said to yourself often, in moments of love or hatred, that you would have a man like dad in your life—or that you definitely wouldn't.

So the feelings about other women and about men that you experienced as a child have a big impact on your capacity to have healthy relationships today. And if that weren't enough, as Black women we must also consider the impact on our relationships of living in a racist, sexist, and class-conscious society.

In *The Power, Passion, and Pain of Black Love*, Jawanza Kunjufu suggests that the values we have learned from Western society make it difficult for Black Americans to have successful, loving relationships.[32] He labels western values "Hip-Hop," and defines the components as individualism, materialism, self-gratification, and immediate and short-term gratification. Kunjufu believes that a more African-centered value system can lead us to stronger relationships, so that maybe one day our divorce rate will fall closer to the five-percent statistic for our sisters and brothers in the Motherland.

The values Kunjufu recommends we embrace are African-centered values based on truth, justice, order, righteousness, harmony, balance, and reciprocity. The search for partners needs to move away from our focus on the external and be based more on shared values. Kunjufu believes that the Hip-Hop approach, which leads to the cash connection and the flesh connection—men seeing women as objects that can be purchased; women sharing their bodies if enough cash is spent on them—will lead to continued frustrations.

> *The values Kunjufu recommends we embrace are African-centered values based on truth, justice, order, righteousness, harmony, balance, and reciprocity.*

This new model of relationship, based on shared values, rests on the idea of love. In his bestseller, *The Road Less Traveled: A New Psychology of Love, Traditional Values and Spiritual Growth*, M. Scott Peck defines love as "the will to extend one's self for the purpose of nurturing one's own or another's spiritual growth."[33] If that quality is absent from our relationships, it is in part because we enter them suffering from what I like to call the Samsonite syndrome: both partners carry with them the heartaches, disappointments, mistakes, rage, and frustrations from prior relationships. The only way to stop carrying such baggage when a relationship ends is to think long and deep about what led to its demise before jumping into yet another doomed relationship. It is only by freeing ourselves from the Samsonite syndrome that we can nurture another person's spiritual growth, because we have learned to nurture our own.

One way that relationships can move toward Peck's definition of love is by setting goals. There should be objectives to strive for in relationships that are larger than the goals of either partner. For example, both of you want children, or both want to grow spiritually. Once a common goal is established, partners may be more willing to compromise for the sake of the relationship, and for the sake of achieving the goal.

Partnering is not for the faint of heart. As Kahlil Gibran notes in *The Prophet*, "For even as love crowns you, so shall he crucify you. Even as he is for your growth, so is he for your pruning."[34]

One way love can be stifled and blocked in relationships is through childhood sexual abuse. It is estimated that as many as one in three women experienced some form of sexual abuse in childhood. Long-term effects may include depression, sexual dysfunction, dissociation, flashbacks, nightmares, numbing of one's feelings, amnesia, feelings of guilt, powerlessness, anger, betrayal, and difficulties with intimacy. Some women are fortunate to avoid significant long-term effects, but

If abuse is part of your history, it is important to gauge how it has affected you and whether you are willing to get help.

many are not. Some women tell and are blamed for the abuse. Other women, who are luckier, received some treatment in childhood that prevented long-term difficulties. If abuse is part of your history, it is important to gauge how it has affected you and whether you are willing to get help.

Given the many tensions that can happen to us, some of us will be unable to make our dreams for a long-term monogamous relationship come true. Relationships have ups and downs, and it takes great patience, faith, and maturity to make them work. People who have shared goals enjoy the harvest of finding and keeping someone able and willing to grow along with them.

But sometimes success isn't in the cards. Then you have to mourn the lost dreams and somehow move on. But how? Are you going to view yourself as incomplete because you don't have a partner? Or are you going to love yourself and become as gratified as you can in other forms of relationships, like friendships or mentoring? If you're looking for a permanent relationship with a child, you can always adopt. My point is that you can live a positive and satisfying life even if you are not romantically involved. It is foolish to sentence yourself to discontent and distress because you can't find the right partner.

Parenting, your relationship with a child, can be as challenging as learning to be a positive partner in a growing relationship. Here, too, not all of us have good training on how to do it well. If we weren't well parented ourselves, how can we start to *be* good parents ourselves?

Parenting is best thought of as stewardship. As Gibran writes in *The Prophet*, "Your children are not your children. They are the sons and daughters of Life's longing for itself. They come through you but not from you, and though they are with you yet they belong not to you."[34] You have to provide a safe and nourishing environment in which a child can grow, till the child can spread her or his wings and fly.

But effective parenting, like effective relationships of any kind, may be inhibited if we bring unresolved disappointments and frustrations from prior relationships. If we continue longing for love and attention, we may seek them from our children instead of listening to their needs. Our goal should be to know our children as the individual human beings they are. We need to facilitate their growth and development. In the process, we are likely to learn about ourselves, and to grow and develop as parents. While we may have dreams for our children, we need to be available to hear, help them discover, and pursue their own dreams.

> *Our goal should be to know our children as the individual human beings they are. We need to facilitate their growth and development. In the process, we are likely to learn about ourselves, and to grow and develop as parents.*

Aleshya Moves On....

Aleshya worked hard to resolve the trauma of her childhood sexual abuse. She was able to identify how keeping the secret and isolating herself from other people inhibited her from establishing intimate relationships. In order to move forward with her life, she had to mourn the loss of a close relationship with her mother and the accompanying sense of abandonment. Because her abuser was dead, she confronted him through role-playing. She continued to work on her issues through a support group for survivors of sexual abuse.

STEPS TO OPTIMUM MENTAL HEALTH

Work on establishing and increasing mutually rewarding relationships with other people, whether friends or a partner. If you have been in an abusive relationship, get help to break the cycle. This involves the courage to recognize your true self and to believe it is "better to have loved and lost, than not to have loved at all."

MORE FOR YOUR HEALTH

Dr. Ann Lightner, in her Sister Sharing Project, and Marilyn Hughes and Gayle K. Porter in their Prime Time Circle of Sister Friends have designed models for women seeking true and supportive sisterhood. Too many Black women are cut off and isolated, simply because they haven't found the resources that help create positive sisterhood. There is truth in our ancestors' words: "Cross the river in a crowd and the crocodile won't eat you."

Books

Lightner, Ann Farrar: *And Your Daughters Shall Preach: Developing a Female Mentoring Program in the African-American Church.* St. Louis: Hodale Press, Inc., 1995.

Gaston, Marilyn Hughes and Gayle K. Porter: *Prime Time: The African American Woman's Complete Guide to Midlife Health and Wellness.* New York: The Ballantine Publishing Group, 2001.

Hooks, Bell: *All About Love*. New York: HarperCollins, 2000.
Richardson, Brenda, and Brenda Wade: *What Mama Couldn't Tell Us About Love*. New York: Harper Collins, 1999.

Movie
Love and Basketball. Positive portrayal of a young couple's struggle with love.

Chapter Nine

There is No Medicine to Cure Hatred

Prejudice and Our Mental Health

Nicole

If Webster's Dictionary needed a photograph to illustrate someone on their last nerve, they could have used Nicole's. Social services had recommended that she get help because they saw that this single mother raising four children was going the wrong way on a one-way street. Nicole was chronically fatigued, she despised her husband for abandoning her, and she was so absorbed by her own internal struggles that she began to neglect her children. The next step would be to lose them.

But Nicole wasn't enthusiastic about treatment. She missed appointments and went for weeks without her antidepressant medication. Ironically, what convinced her to go on medication and stay there was an act of racial prejudice. One day, she stormed into my office enraged, and demanded that I see her immediately. An older Asian boy at school had called her six-year-old daughter "nigger" and Nicole was ready to kill him. If she didn't get some "nerve pills," she was going to do it, she swore.

HOW PREJUDICE COMES ABOUT

For many of us, day to day experiences of racial prejudice can be what bring us down to our last nerves. Black Americans sometimes find it hard to decide which is more American, hatred or apple pie. Blacks in America have been recipients of a dangerous human tendency we call hatred of the other, which goes back to Cain and Abel. Hatred and the *isms* associated with it are facts of life that many Black people face every day. But what is not written in stone is how we respond to it, and, especially, how to avoid internalizing it.

As always, learning to change the way we respond means learning to be attentive to the way we respond now. Has there been a time when you were in conversation and you heard the words, "You people?" Other than blatant epithets, few words have as great an alarm potential as "you people." They alert us that we are in the presence of someone who does not recognize us as individuals. The words also elicit our fight or flight response. We find ourselves in the direct presence of racism, or sexism, or homophobia, or any other distorted way of viewing us. If we don't learn to manage other people's hatred and, yes, stupidity, when we bump into them, we can be deeply wounded, and left with feelings of anxiety, depression, or even posttraumatic stress disorder.

Although racism, sad to say, has an ancient history, Dr. Willie Hamlin of Washington, DC believes that it is a disease and should be viewed as a mental disorder. [35] Let's take a look at the origins of racism, prejudice—this *disease*—and how it develops.

Early on, as infants, we don't know that we are separate human beings. The child doesn't know the difference between herself and other people. Over the first several months of life, we begin to discover this difference through the many frustrations we can encounter in satisfying our needs. We begin to understand that our needs are not fulfilled automatically, and that we are separate from our caretakers. We learn that we must use everything in our power to communicate, usually through crying, what we need and want.

After we've mastered crawling and walking, our sense of separateness becomes real. In the course of this development, we become aware of how much is in our environment and needs to become known. That's a lot of information for a little mind to process, and the child learns to do this complicated job by organizing similar things, like colors, or classes of objects, into groupings.

One of the first and most important distinctions we make is between what is known and unknown. Within our families we acquire the ability to distinguish what is familiar and what is not. "Oh, that's Aunt Phyllis. She comes every week." Familiar becomes good to us. We don't have to expend energy getting to know the familiar. But strangers require us to use energy to distinguish whether they are helpful or harmful. Non-familiar becomes bad just because it is inconvenient and requires work on our part.

As this process of sorting continues, the people around us encourage us to develop a sense of loyalty and identity. We like the people we are with and to whom we are similar. They are our "in" group; others are the "out" group. Fears and insecurities about the "other" lead us to cling to people who are like us. We also tend to project unwanted aspects of ourselves or our family members onto the "other." Through these processes, with the assistance of our group and the larger culture, we develop a sense of our own value or worth compared to others.

Mainstream culture in America tends to devalue every group except heterosexual white men. In *Black Skins, White Masks*, the Algerian psychiatrist Frantz Fanon argued that all Blacks who develop in a racist society take in some of this negative stereotyping and direct it towards themselves.[48] This process can impact any group which is not valued by the larger society, be it women, the poor, or homosexuals. In each case, the possibility of turning cultural prejudice into self-hatred is real.

We have seen that prejudice has two components: the grouping of individuals, and assigning many of those groups a negative value. Prejudice is entrenched and hard to uproot because it is born of natural inclinations. We must decide how to deal with prejudice in order to minimize its negative impact. Only by doing so can we have a chance of succeeding in the larger community.

As things stand, we usually cannot directly attack the larger community, so we hurt ourselves or the people closest to ourselves. If a father is full of rage and frustration, or a mother without any sense of her self-worth, what are the chances that their children will grow up to be mentally and emotionally healthy adults? If children have a test in school the morning after a horrific night of abuse, how well are they likely to perform? How will they raise their own children?

I remember seeing an editorial cartoon that depicted a Klansman reading a newspaper article about black-on-black homicide, and he was wearing a huge grin. The Klansman no longer had to perpetrate crimes against us, because we were doing a good job of it ourselves.

LEAVING OUR RAGE AT THE DOOR

To leave our rage at the door, so that we do not turn it against ourselves and the people we love, we must first acknowledge that we are enraged. Sometimes we are so fearful of our wrath that we try to deny how we really feel. We want to avoid the feelings of helplessness and hopelessness and the sense of being trapped. We sometimes fear acknowledging the rage because we believe it is so immense it could destroy us or the people around us. This fear is particularly true for people who have been abused as children or for prisoners who were tortured or tormented in some way. Any current aggression toward us may force us to relive an experience that was terrifying in the past when we did not have the size or skills to protect ourselves.

But denying these feelings of rage doesn't allow us to find successful outlets for it. Most bathtubs come with an extra drain, always open and near the top. If someone leaves the water running, that safety drain will keep the tub from overflowing. Imagine having a tub without a safety drain and the consequences of soaked floors. In a similar way, letting your rage overflow will cost you dearly.

It isn't surprising that some studies connect racism with high blood pressure. If we are continuously hyper-vigilant, we are continuously releasing adrenaline, that fight-or-flight hormone that increases our heart rate and our blood pressure when we are faced with threats. If you keep the feelings bottled up, you can emotionally explode, or become a substance abuser or start eating too much, or suffer from the many ailments associated with high blood pressure.

One reason that people act out their anger is to avoid the uncomfortable feeling of helplessness. Women as well as men try to ease their pain by using aggression and even violence to make other people feel as miserable as they do. This process of making someone else feel what we don't want to feel happens rapidly and outside our awareness. It's a kind of panic response associated with feelings of helplessness. Mental health workers call this process "turning passive into active"; we hurt to avoid feeling hurt and helpless.

> *We hurt to avoid feeling hurt and helpless.*

While prejudice works through individuals, it is a public problem, and government and businesses work to correct it through diversity training. Our workplaces have become more diverse, and, for the majority of us, they are the major points of contact we have with people of different races, sexual orientation, and economic status. Several successful class action lawsuits have also contributed to a new public interest in understanding differences. While progress in this area is slow, there has been progress.

Yet the task remains: only by looking at yourself in the mirror can you overcome your own prejudices. It's a task each of us must complete before we can work to end the problem of social prejudice and injustice in the larger society. Can you see your own prejudices, such as sexism and homophobia, and learn to heal them? Equally important, can you recognize how you have internalized racism and self-hatred and direct them against yourself?

While the prejudice other people direct against us may be slow to change, we do have the power to heal self-hatred by working toward positive Black identity. W. E. Cross, Jr. presents the stages we must go through in order to embrace Black identity:[37]

- *Pre-encounter:* The individual idealizes the dominant White worldview of superiority and devaluation of Blacks. She disassociates herself from Blacks, using Whites as her point of reference. She is successful and views herself as being different from other Blacks. Denial is employed to screen out evidence that she is not part of the "in" racial group. She might join an all-White country club, and in the locker room one day a member, thinking she is the help, asks her to get her a towel. She downplays the significance of this experience.
- *Encounter:* In this stage, events shatter the façade of denial, and the individual understands that she will be seen as Black and inferior by Whites. This understanding is the beginning of a journey toward a new identity, and it releases a range of feelings: confusion, anxiety, hopelessness, anger, depression—but also euphoria. Having shed her previous identity, she actively seeks a new Black identity.
- *Immersion/Emmersion:* During the Immersion stage the individual thinks, feels, and acts the way she believes

"authentic" Black Americans do. She embraces the stereotypical. She becomes angry at Whites because of racial oppression. She idealizes Blacks and denigrates Whites. Emmersion involves moving past stereotypical Blackness to acceptance of Blackness, toward an ability to see the strengths and weaknesses of being Black and of Black culture itself. The individual is less dependent on other people's definition of Blackness for a sense of self-worth.

- *Internalization:* In this stage the individual is able to combine who she is individually with a positive and personally relevant Black identity. Her reference group becomes other Black Americans. Personally strong, she can now decide on how she will deal with Whites. She no longer idealizes Whiteness or White culture, seeing both its weaknesses and strengths. If she chooses to, she can reestablish relationships with Whites who, in her view, are enlightened.

Nicole Moves On....

After Nicole stomped into my office, upset over the racial epithet hurled at her daughter, she calmed down with several deep breaths and talked about her rage. With exploration, she was able to connect her current rage with her own experience of being called "nigger" in elementary school. She had responded then by fighting and was suspended. She cried when she recognized that she was also feeling inadequate as a parent because she had been unable to protect her daughter from experiencing a hurt similar to her own.

In this session, we worked on developing a less destructive

An Exercise

1. Write the stages of Black racial identity in your journal. Try to identify your personal experiences with each stage. Did you have experiences that made you see the light? What stage do you see yourself in now? Do you need to develop further?

2. Are there racial experiences you still struggle with? Are they interfering with daily life more than you would like? Explore why these particular experiences have hurt you so much and commit yourself to decreasing their hold on you.

   A Zen story recounts that two monks are traveling when they come upon a stream they must cross to continue on their journey. A young woman stands on the bank and wants to cross without getting wet. Although their faith forbids them from touching a woman, one of the monks carries her across the stream and leaves her safely on the other side. The two monks continue on their journey in silence. Hours later, the monk who witnessed the other one carrying the woman inquires about his act. The monk replies, "I have long since put the woman down, but you obviously continue to carry her." What are you ready to put down?

3. What can you commit yourself to do that will make a difference in decreasing hatred and prejudice in your community?

continued on next page

continued from previous page

With a strong sense of female and racial identity, we can begin to focus our energies on making a difference. Harnessing your anger and directing it toward constructive activities is crucial to our freedom and mental health. Joining the NAACP, demonstrating for something you believe in, or participating in letter-writing campaigns are options that will increase your sense of empowerment. Identify the activities you are willing to do or the organizations you are willing to work for. Such commitment will relieve your sense of hopelessness and helplessness by teaching you that you don't have to be Superwoman to do something in your own behalf.

reaction than harming the boy. She decided she needed to listen better to what her daughter had to say about the experience instead of reacting to her own past hurts, and to try to help her daughter understand how other people tried to make her feel bad because of their own insecurities. She also planned to talk to the principal about the incident and to find out what the school policy was on handling similar incidents.

Because this session was supportive therapy, she was encouraged to begin reading her children books that affirm Black Americans and our culture. She was also encouraged to keep her appointments. We had more work to do.

STEPS TO OPTIMUM MENTAL HEALTH

Commit yourself to identifying ways you may have internalized self-hatred, for whatever reason. Work with a therapist, minister, or close friend on healing from past traumas related to sexism, racism, and heterosexism.

Identify at least one activity you are willing to do, or one organization you are willing to work for, to increase tolerance in your community. Check your anger at the door.

MORE FOR YOUR HEALTH
Book
Morrison,Toni: *The Bluest Eye*. New York: Alfred A. Knopf, 1970. The struggles of racial identity are addressed.

Movie
Bamboozled. Demonstrates the destructive nature of racial hatred, whether by Whites or Blacks.

CHAPTER TEN

WHEN ONE IS IN TROUBLE, ONE REMEMBERS GOD

The Role of Spirituality in Mental Health

Linda

Linda was dying from AIDS. Her shame drove her into a deep depression and she found it agonizing to speak of the stress in her life. Along with the many drugs she needed to combat the deadly virus, she also took an antidepressant. Yet, she frequently had thoughts of taking her own life. When we met in therapy, she told me she had come close to committing suicide the night before. I asked what had kept her from following through, and she replied, without hesitation, "I believe in God."

"*I found God in myself & I loved her/ I loved her fiercely.*" These words from Ntozake Shange's poignant play, *For Colored Girls who have Considered Suicide/When the Rainbow is Enuf,* capture how closely entwined spirituality is to the essence of Black women. A popular adage goes that while the religious practice their religion because they fear that if they don't, they will go

169

to hell, the spiritual person has already been there. Given the challenges many of us face, we can be called *seriously* spiritual.

That's why we can't talk about *Saving Our Last Nerve* without exploring spirituality. The connection between spirituality and mental health is widely recognized in both the public and private sectors. Increasingly, people who fund mental health services are devoting more dollars to the study of the relationship between mental health and faith.

The Center for Mental Health Services in Rockville, Maryland funded a model project called "Healing the Brokenhearted: The Faith Community Responds to Depression in 1999." Headed by Dr. Eleanor Bryant, pastor of Agape Fellowship Church in Randallstown, Maryland, the project's goal was to create an environment where the mental health and faith communities could educate each other about their respective contributions to mental health. Mental health professionals needed to understand that many Black Americans turned to the church when life became unbearable, and they needed to know how the clergy responded. The religious community, in turn, needed to understand the many treatment options provided by mental health services. The hope is that other communities will establish similar programs.

Why was such a project necessary? Misconceptions and sometimes even a sense of competition have contributed to a divide between mental health and spiritual resources. To address that divide, I often present a lecture entitled: *What to Take on the Journey: God, Zoloft or Both?* When I give this lecture, I hope my audience will learn that a holistic approach to achieving mental health is the best approach.

But the deep distrust between the faith and mental health

communities has been a barrier against accepting that approach. Of course, mental health professionals have sometimes thrown gasoline on the fire by badmouthing religion. Drs. William Grier and Price Cobbs, Black American psychiatrists and co-authors of *The Jesus Bag*, are prime examples.[38] In their book, they argue that religion encourages Black Americans to remain law-abiding, passive, and in a state of denial about their rage. These authors see religion as encouraging Blacks to accept their oppression and deprivation in this world and to focus their hopes on salvation in the next one. Dr. Sigmund Freud, the founder of psychoanalysis, also wrote that religion was an illusion which people engaged in to avoid facing the harsh realities of life. Many patients have said that when they spoke about religious issues, mental health providers considered them crazy.

On the other side, many patients in therapy have reported that their clergy suggested their difficulties were caused by a lack of faith, or demons. Some church leaders have even encouraged their members to avoid psychiatric medications and treatment. I find it interesting that if a church member has been seriously ill with a physical condition, recovers, and returns to church, the minister and the congregation publicly praise her. But if a church member is stricken by severe depression and eventually recovers, her welcome back isn't nearly as openly celebrated. So we see that both the mental health and faith communities have often neglected what is best for the individual—a holistic approach to care.

Few Black American women leave childhood without carrying these words in their hearts from one of my favorite gospels: "This little light of mine, I'm going to let it shine."

Many of us were raised in church-going families. In fact, the majority of Americans—about 90 percent, according to Gallup polls—report a belief in God or a higher power.

The recent interest in the impact of spirituality on a person's overall health has brought a discovery—something African and Eastern cultures have always understood—that our health and well-being are intimately tied to our faith. In one African tribe, the woman is both a healer *and* a spiritual leader.

African and Eastern cultures have always understood that our health and well-being are intimately tied to our faith.

Renita Weems, a biblical scholar, notes in her essay, "Reading Her Way Through the Struggle: African-American Women in the Bible," (in *Stony the Road We Trod: African American Biblical Interpretation*) that many Black American women have learned to focus on components of religion and the Bible that validate themselves.[39] Weems sees this focus as a reaction to the slave master who prevented slaves from reading the Bible so he could interpret it in support of oppression. Many sisters are unwilling to endorse any aspect of religion that goes against their basic survival instincts.

In studying the impact spirituality has on our health, researchers have divided believers into people who see religion as an end in itself and people who see it as a means to an end. The first group of believers they call "intrinsic," the second, "extrinsic." The first group worships God and benefits primarily from their relationship with a Supreme Being. The second group finds more direct value in the social benefits of belonging to a particular congregation. These same researchers find that intrinsic believers are likely to enjoy better health and recover better if they fall ill than extrinsic believers. They are also likely to enjoy a stronger sense of well being.

Faith and prayer may also benefit one's health. A study by Christian cardiologist Randoph Byrd found that patients who were prayed for needed significantly fewer antibiotics and were less likely to develop pulmonary edema (increased fluid in the lungs), or to need an artificial airway, than patients who were not prayed for.[40]

But incorporating spirituality into believers' lives is not always beneficial. Dr. Michele Balamani, a psychologist, addressed the subject of depression in Black American Christian women and came up with some surprising conclusions.[41] Keeping busy with church work and being overly spiritual, she found, are common masks used by Black, churchgoing, Christian women. And masking our wounds, though a socially acceptable deception, is psychologically and theologically unsound. Masking the wounds of our oppression limits real (right) relationships with God, self, and others and the peace and joy that are products of right relationships.

A Russian proverb advises, "Pray to God, but row for the shore." This proverb reminds me of a frequently told tale: A flood is slowly swallowing a Midwestern town and one fellow, a man of strong faith, looks out the window of his home as a rowboat passes by. The water is up to the man's knees. The boat owner asks him if he wants a ride. "No," he replies, "I'm waiting for God to rescue me."

The water continues to rise and the believer moves up to the second floor and sees a motor boat passing. The driver, spotting the man through the window, offers him a ride. Again he responds, "I'm waiting on the Lord to rescue me." Finally, the water rises further and it is necessary for the believer to climb onto the roof. A helicopter flies overhead and drops a ladder but he again shouts to the pilot that he's waiting on the Lord.

Soon, the water rises again, and the believer is swept away, drowns, and arrives at the Pearly Gates. Once in the Lord's presence, he protests bitterly about his early death. He tells God, "I prayed for you to rescue me. Why didn't you?" God replies, "Who do you think sent the two boats and the helicopter?"

Some of us are certain we have been abandoned by God when things don't go as smoothly as we would like—perhaps an example of our past jumping into today's business. Some of us see the Higher Being as we saw our parents. If they were unreliable, our God may also seem unreliable. Spiritual growth helps us to begin to view God outside the bounds of our relationship with our parents. Yes, some of us have had negative experiences with organized religion, but these shouldn't prevent us from continuing on our spiritual journeys in other ways.

How *do* spiritually active people experience the presence of God in their daily lives? Dr. Kenneth Pargament divides the coping styles of spiritually-inclined people into three categories:[42]

- self-directing
- collaborative
- deferring

Let's see how this might work in practice. Say you have learned that your employer will soon lay off half the office. Since you just started nine months ago, you expect to lose your job. If you are a *self-directing* woman, instead of despairing, you believe that God has supplied you with all you need to find a new job. You search the want ads, query friends and colleagues for leads. Chances are, it won't be long before you land another job.

If you are a *collaborative* woman, you pray for guidance as you update your resume, choose an outfit for an interview, and go over your answers to the ten questions the interviewer will most likely ask. You believe that, with God's help and some elbow grease on your part, you will be successful.

Finally, if you are a *deferring* woman, you find yourself praying consistently that employment will come to you through divine intervention. You are ready to wait on the Lord and be of good courage.

The model you use may change depending on what challenge you face. You may use the collaborative mode when preparing for an exam. A person in the last stages of a terminal illness may pray in a deferring fashion.

As I mentioned earlier in this chapter, there is proof that faith can heal. One study compared two groups of patients hospitalized for depression. One group was religious; the other was not. The believers recovered sooner from their depression.

H. C. Meserve maintains that religion has healing powers because it encourages self-knowledge and self-acceptance.[43] Our religious beliefs help us work toward ideals and goals and lead more responsible and healthier lives. We can develop new resiliency and adaptive skills to handle crises and conflicts. Religion, Meserve says, gives order to lives which otherwise might be haphazard or chaotic. The church helps contribute to health by supporting its members in times of sorrow and need, and also provides a network of concerned people.

> *Remember, the benefits of religion are greater for people who love spirituality for itself than for people who participate solely for extrinsic reasons.*

Do you have to go out and find religion to have a healthier life? Well, it won't hurt. But remember, the benefits of religion are greater for people who love spirituality for itself than for people who participate solely for extrinsic reasons.

Healthy spirituality should help us cope with our anxieties and give us the means to master life's challenges. Our beliefs can lead us to develop a personal relationship with God, and through God find the help to confront the sources of our fears and insecurities. If we do not learn to confront the tasks before us, we cannot truly learn to take care of ourselves and we will forever seek external nurturing. If we *do* face these challenges, we will come to know our strengths and find the conviction to lead healthy lives.

What lies behind us and before us is minuscule compared to what lies within us. What lies within us is spirit in human form. Sometimes our suffering makes us forget that we are fueled by something greater than our human energy. We sing, "This little light of mine" because we know that light is precious, not of our making, and can sustain us even in the darkness.

When you are stressed or depressed, you may lose sight of

your faith. You may lose focus, and that's where mental health care professionals can help.

An Exercise

Spend some time over a period of a week or two reflecting on the following, and writing down your thoughts in a journal.

· What do I believe in?
· If I belong to a particular denomination, what aspects of its doctrine are most alive to me?
· What religious beliefs did my parents and grandparents hold, and why did they hold these beliefs?
· What is the meaning of my life?
· What am I trying to accomplish to fulfill that meaning?
· Do I still hold to religious "beliefs" that no longer fulfill me?
· What is my God like?
· What possible hurts do I still carry from past religious experiences? Do these old wounds block my spiritual growth?

If it is important to you, explore your spirituality further, through organized religion, a spiritual director, or your own study.

Linda Moves On....

Not only was Linda an AIDS patient who suffered from depression, but she was also a drug addict. The goal of our work together was to help her live her remaining days fully and try to come to terms with her death. She and I found the work difficult, and she returned to drug abuse, especially when she experienced fear and emotional distress. Yet, even in the final stages of her illness, she continued to trust in God.

STEPS TO OPTIMUM MENTAL HEALTH

It has been said that we are all sent to earth with sealed orders. It is our responsibility, while we are here, to open, decipher, and then fulfill these orders. Have you discovered yours?

MORE FOR YOUR HEALTH

Books

LaBelle, Patti: *Don't Block the Blessing.* New York: Riverhead Books, 1996.

Kaufer, Nelly, and Carol Osmer-Newhouse: *A Woman's Guide to Spiritual Renewal.* New York: Harper Collins, 1994.

Hull, Akasha Gloria: *The New Spirituality of African-American Women.* Rochester, Vermont: Inner Traditions International, 2001.

Movies

The Preacher's Wife, The Robe, and *The Apostle* address the importance of spirituality in the characters' lives.

Chapter Eleven

It is Only the Water that is Spilt; the Calabash is not Broken

The Future is Ours to Create

Phyllis

For the past twenty-three years, Phyllis has risen at five a.m. to exercise with the television instructor. When Phyllis broke her hip ten years ago, she healed quickly because she was in such excellent shape. A few years later, thyroid cancer required surgery and years of medication, yet she continues living her life to the fullest. It's been thirty years since her boyfriend died; forty since her husband passed on. The last of her six siblings was buried five years ago, and the friends who have departed are too numerous to count. It wasn't God's will for her to have children, but she has helped raise a platoon of nieces and nephews. She has buried several of them, as well. The nursing home where she has volunteered for the last twenty-four years has honored her several times. She has been an active member of her Baptist church for the past fifty years, missing services only when she was traveling. She says she saved her last nerve all these years by valuing herself enough to take care of herself, counting all her blessings, and loving and serving God.

She is an inspiration to me and to the many people she has touched. She is not a patient. Phyllis is my eighty-nine-year-old aunt.

We have had hard times in this country, but the journey is not finished. Whether we are talking about depression, economic hardship, or the fallout from years of racial oppression, each day we must decide how to live with challenges. Throughout this book, I have invited you to re-examine your past. It is now time to come to terms with what happened yesterday, and step onto the path that leads to better mental health in the future. Hopefully, you have gained knowledge about your coping styles and have taken the time to develop a personalized stress management plan. Remember, change doesn't happen overnight. Change is an on-going process involving daily choices that will eventually lead you to Optimum Mental Health.

As we travel on the path to Optimum Mental Health, we need to continually expand our internal and external resources, so that we can love and live our lives as enjoyably and fully as possible.

Years ago, in kindergarten, we learned our ABCs. They served as the building blocks for a world of new words that provided us with information to empower our lives. By reading this book, you have improved your mental health literacy and can take the necessary steps to *save your last nerve.*

The following ABCs of Mental Health for African Americans can serve as the building blocks for Optimum Mental Health. While you may not currently possess all of these attributes, working toward them will enable you to begin living a healthier life. As we travel on the path to Optimum Mental Health, we need to continually expand our internal and external resources, so that we can love and live our lives as enjoyably and fully as possible.

THE ABC'S OF IT
A

Able: We need to claim our power and skills, offering them to ourselves and to the people we love. We are here to invest time and energy in discovering and developing our capabilities.

Active: Our mental and physical health is tied to our level of physical activity. Increasing our daily activity has positive rewards for us. *Active* also means that life is not happening to us; rather, we embrace and live life to its fullest. There are times when we must also be activists, whether for better education for our children or as volunteers at a food bank.

Affirming: Declaring positively who we are and who we shall be is the first step in getting there. The minimum daily requirement of affirmation is at least one affirming statement to ourselves and to the people with whom we journey.

Angry: Our mental health depends on coming to terms with our anger. We all experience anger, and trying to deny it leaves us vulnerable to the negative physical and emotional effects of its buildup. Black American women need to develop healthy ways of dealing with anger.

B

Believing: Trusting in the goodness of ourselves and whatever Higher Power we embrace leads us forward on our journey.

Birthing: Each day we are born anew. If we are willing to let go of what we were yesterday and embrace new possibilities, we will always be able to have new dreams and relationships.

Bright: "This little light of mine, I'm going to let it shine." Remaining in touch with who we truly are is an everlasting resource we can draw upon in the most challenging moments. Untreated depression and other illnesses dim our inner light, the sense of who we are, and our potential.

C

Called: We are summoned to live our lives for a purpose. What are you called to do? Identifying your calling and working toward it leads to gratification and inner peace when you are at your journey's end.

Caring: We must be invested in looking after ourselves and the people we love. Remember what they say on every flight? "In case of an emergency and a drop in cabin pressure, people traveling with small children should first put on their own oxygen masks and then their children's masks." Ongoing positive self-care is a strong indication of mental health. Self-care is not selfish, it is essential.

Committed: We need to feel comfortable binding ourselves to our families, our nation, our relationships, our Higher Power, and ourselves. Once we decide on our commitments, we can unleash our inner power.

Competent: A sense of being lovable and capable is the solid rock on which healthy self-esteem rests. Continually work on the career and interpersonal skills you want to develop. Moving toward the goals we set for ourselves boosts our positive self-regard and increases the resources we can give to the community. Providing positive feedback to our children gives them the foundation and courage to take the bigger steps they will need on their life's journey.

D

Daring: In our lives, there will come a time when courage is required: picking up the phone and making an appointment with a therapist, confronting a teacher that is treating your child unfairly, or leaving an abusive relationship. Helen Keller told us, "Life is a daring adventure, or nothing at all."

Developing: We're getting older and getting better. This classroom of life expects us to be continuously studying and doing our homework. Ongoing mental stimulation keeps us from becoming stagnant.

Doing: While there is a time for rest, there is also a time for doing. After the planning, the praying, the talking, it is time to just do it! It is essential to take action to achieve our goals.

E

Empowered: Wasn't it the Isley Brothers who loudly sang, "You've got the Power!"? Optimum Mental Health allows us to realistically assess what we can do. With knowledge of our true ability, we won't sell ourselves short or live in grandiosity. We need to be empowered and also empower the people around us. Helping our loved ones acknowledge and use their abilities leaves us free to develop and use ours.

Enduring: Sometimes we must just hold up and hold on. Those months of sleepless nights with a newborn, or those long weeks of chemotherapy treatments challenge us. During these periods, we need prayer partners, friends, and healers. We have to release our fantasy of going it alone and reach out for help without shame. When others are enduring alone, we need to reach out and let them know that interdependence is the best solution for all of us.

Energetic: When we have successfully grieved our losses or received treatment for our depression, we can return to our true selves. We can tap into our life energy, discover what we are here to accomplish, and achieve it.

Enjoying: To be able to experience pleasure speaks well for our mental health. It means we have come to a workable compromise with the part of us that tells us what is right and wrong (our conscience), and the part that would risk everything for a good time. It means that depression and anxiety are no longer able to steal our joy.

F

Faithful: Faith has served our people well. We have continued to believe without concrete evidence and moved many a mountain. Whether we are speaking of faith in ourselves, a Higher Power, or just saying that good will triumph over evil, faith keeps us creating new possibilities.

Focused: Untreated depression, anxiety, or psychotic disorders all can impair our ability to pay attention to work, school, family, or spiritual development. Without focus, we are unable to achieve the goals we set for ourselves.

Forgiving: Our resentment against ourselves and others can become like a prison. Forgiving may best be thought of as an ongoing process as opposed to an act that is completed immediately. Forgiving involves our ability to identify the actual disappointment we experienced, along with what was lost and associated dreams. Forgiving ourselves for being less than perfect is a great commitment, maybe even harder than forgiving others. Therapy can successfully address long-term resentments that hurt our interpersonal relationships and our ability to forgive.

G

Gifted: What is your talent or natural ability? What are you doing with it? Are you allowing self-criticism to get in the way of developing your gift? As you decrease your tendency to defeat yourself before the game even begins, wondrous things will happen in your life.

Giving: To share our love, joy, skills, intellect, humor, compassion, anger, and forgiveness with other people, we must be willing to know and accept ourselves. Giving without undue sacrifice demonstrates our belief that we have something that is desired or needed and that we are worthwhile. People who give little or too much may have internal struggles with self-worth, or a sense of depletion or inadequacy. Spiritual sisters understand that giving to other people is actually giving to themselves.

Growing: As Black American women, we want to be able to move past survival and thrive. We're aiming to reach our fullest potential.

H

Healing: We will continuously experience disappointment, loss, and major and minor wounds to our bodies, minds, and spirits. Healing involves moving toward becoming whole again. Ernest Hemingway wrote in *A Farewell to Arms:* "Life breaks everyone, and afterwards, some of us are strong in the broken places." [48] We will have some battle scars, but we heal when we move forward instead of remaining stuck.

Healthy: To the best of our abilities, we must strive toward physical, mental, and spiritual health. Even if we are diagnosed with illness, we must make decisions that are in our best interests. We have to live in each moment but also make choices that will increase our likelihood of good health in the future.

Helping: Being useful to other people adds to our positive self-regard. Serving other people allows us to move from focusing on our own challenges to being aware of our larger community.

Hoping: Mental health allows us to desire and expect a positive outcome. Hopelessness is often a symptom of depression that can eventually lead to self-injurious acts. It is important to get help before your situation becomes overwhelming. Getting such help is a basic act of self-respect and self-reverence.

I

Ingenuous: We must move out of secrecy and become open and frank about matters that are important to our health and happiness. We need to educate ourselves about our sexuality and unashamedly pass this information on to our younger sisters. Physical, sexual, and emotional abuse thrives on silence. Telling the truth will set us free.

Interested: Concern for our health and well-being demonstrates healthy self-esteem. Black American women need to be committed to obtaining the latest information on health promotion and illness prevention. We can no longer afford to ignore harmful behaviors, saying good care is for White girls. We are the ones dying early from diabetes, heart disease, AIDS, high blood pressure, and complications from obesity.

Involved: Whether it be our work, our home life, our faith, our politics, involvement signals we are able to manage our internal demands well enough to have energy left over for work, love, play, and creativity.

J

Joyful: Joy to the world. If we give ourselves permission, our journey through life will be as gratifying as we wish it to be. Untreated mental illness and ongoing stress steal joy. We can choose it to be otherwise, but only if we feel we are worthy of joy.

Judicious: Sound judgment keeps us out of harmful situations and relationships. We need to feel comfortable doing reality checks. Impairment of judgment by chronic substance abuse has caused the demise of many sisters.

K

Kind: We must be gentle and benevolent toward ourselves. Some of us are quite good at showing kindness toward other people and making hostile attacks on ourselves. Mental health involves embracing ourselves with kindness and care.

L

Laughing: The ability to laugh lovingly at ourselves and to find the humor in life promotes health. Your local comedy club or even a good humorous book can be a great source of stress management. Humor that humiliates other people, on the other hand, can be quite damaging.

Learning: Continually seeking to know more about ourselves and the world around us enables us to be equipped for new and greater challenges. We need to learn how to cope more effectively instead of hoping all our troubles will disappear.

Loving: Healthy loving involves knowing and accepting our true selves. Narcissism involves being caught up with an image or ideal of the self, as opposed to the true self. Loving ourselves enables us to care for ourselves.

M

Meditating: Focusing on and listening to your inner self keeps you aware of what is really important, and allows you to remain connected to that inner place of beauty, truth, peace, and love.

Mindful: Strive to be present and aware of the moment, so that you can experience each day to its fullest. Dwelling excessively on the past or the future limits your ability to appreciate the here and now.

Moving: Traveling through life without dwelling on past hurts and disappointments should be our goal. We don't have to deny the pain; simply put it in its place in the context of our current reality.

N

Needful: With Optimum Mental Health, we can acknowledge all our needs, whether for closeness, affirmation, help, or quiet. Post this warning on your mirror: ***Denial of Needs can be Hazardous to my Mental Health.***

Nurturing: It is time to nourish ourselves and other people. In order to continue to grow and develop, we, like houseplants, require some tender care. It is time for us to give ourselves positive feedback, and surround ourselves with other people for whom we care and who genuinely care for us. Without hesitation, we will be able to say, "I love you" to our partners, sister friends, and ourselves.

O

Opportunistic: If we are healthy, we can take advantage of opportunities when they arise. If we have successfully addressed our self-defeating attitudes, inhibitions can't keep us from opportunities. If we have resolved the pains of old relationships, we can try again when potential partners appear in our lives.

Overcoming: We shall overcome. To do so, we need the ability to see and move past current challenges. Realistically appraising a situation allows us to gather the necessary resources to achieve the desired outcome.

P

Persistent: We must not let depression or other conditions keep us from identifying, and then going wholeheartedly after, our goals.

Powerful: It is desirable to become more comfortable with how power-filled we really are. If we give ourselves permission to be all we can be, we will recognize that, though there are some people who may seek to limit us, we usually inhibit ourselves the most.

Praising: We can go about acknowledging our worth, as well as the worth of other people and our Higher Power. We are healthy enough to identify the good in ourselves without dwelling on the negative or aggrandizing.

Prayerful: We are comfortable asking for assistance, guidance, and serenity, as well as being able to praise.

Precious: Honoring ourselves as the precious and unique creations we are signals healthy self-regard. Like diamonds created by years of pressure, we need to value our life experiences for the lessons they have taught us. We are jewels because of the challenges we have met head-on and survived.

Q

Quiet: Be still. Being unafraid to really be with yourself enables you to listen for "your still small voice." Allow yourself to become aware of what you are truly feeling, whether it is anger, joy, fear, love, or grief.

R

Reaching: The ability to strive for a healthy self, relationship, or fulfilling career, so that we have a full account of who we are in this moment, are unafraid, and are eager to develop ourselves further.

Ready: We are unhindered, prepared, and willing to act. It is time that we take action to protect Our Last Nerve.

Resting: Even God rested on the seventh day. Rest allows us to rejuvenate ourselves. If we go too long without appropriate rest, we can get burned out. Sleep disturbance is one of the symptoms of depression and mania.

Rising: Seek to ascend from the valleys in life. There is a season for sadness, but only a season. When we are unable to arise on our own, we need to seek assistance from our spiritual leaders, therapists, or doctors.

S

Seeking: What we know encourages us to learn even more. We yearn to know ourselves more completely, and seek to be in relationships with other people.

Sexual: We need to grant ourselves permission to rejoice in our sexuality. Mental health allows us to feel pleasure and to be equally concerned with giving and receiving sexual satisfaction. We are also comfortable exercising personal decisions about our sexuality, whether that is saying yes or no.

Sincere: We abandon our attempts to deceive ourselves and other people. Say good-bye to the pretense of joy when we are really angry and to the pretense of anger when we are really hurting inside.

Sistering: We celebrate our relationships with women. We take advantage of opportunities to unashamedly rejoice in who we are as the female energy of the universe. Whether we give birth to children or not, we provide nourishment and affirmation to other people. Doing so is healthy so long as we do not neglect ourselves in the process and act out of conscious choice.

Spiritual: We are able to explore life's meaning, and discover some meaning in our existence. We seek to understand the connection between ourselves and other people and gain some knowledge of our souls. We may come to believe that we are all spiritual beings in human form.

T

Tearful: There is a season for laughter and a season for tears. It is healthy to cry when we hurt, to be able to acknowledge the loss we are experiencing. Many of us have reservoirs of tears waiting to drain from us, if only we will allow them to be released. The World Trade Center and Pentagon disasters made many of us cry for the people directly affected, and for ourselves. Crying, or, as I say, sweating of the eyeballs, is a natural function, so who are we to get in the way of nature?

U

Unapologetic: Wallowing in regret for who we are, or what we have done, takes energy away from our current abilities. Yes, where you've hurt and disappointed others and yourself, make amends where you can, sincerely and openly. Then move forward, knowing that if you have made unwise choices, you now have the strength to choose differently.

Unstoppable: We're on the move. Get out of our way! Mental health or bust!

V

Valuing: We must continue to value ourselves, our families, and our friends. We must identify the values we will live by.

Victorious: We can be triumphant in our struggles. Hopelessness and helplessness were not meant to be our permanent companions.

W

Waging war: Untreated mental illnesses can ruin and even end our lives. Reading this book and other material on mental illnesses and mental health is an act of war. It's time for a war on ignorance about this essential part of us.

Wanting: We can move past just wanting our needs met, and identify what we desire in life. We need not be ashamed of natural desires for sexual gratification, or other desires for closeness. We can want more than just to survive. We want to thrive.

Willing: We must agree to take the necessary steps to Save Our Last Nerve, by identifying the sources of our stress and developing a personal game plan. We must participate in our own rescue.

X

XX: We have two x chromosomes, essential to being female. We can celebrate who we are as women by strutting a little. If no one else celebrates you, celebrate yourself! You may be surprised to find that soon others will follow suit.

Y

Yes: It is important that we are able to say "yes" to ourselves—to our dreams, our possibilities, to all that we encounter on the journey. Some things may not be to our liking, but they are all part of life. It is up to us to accept the good and bad that we cannot control, bend when we must, and stand firm when it is called for. Yes, we can cope with life.

Z

Zealous: Let us live with intense enthusiasm. We are making this journey only once. We are on stage. This is not a dress rehearsal. Let's play each and every scene to the greatest extent possible.

May you take the necessary steps to Optimum Mental Health. You can do it!

Notes

1. *Minorities and Mental Health: A Report of the Surgeon General.* Rockville, MD, 1:1.

2. S. Johnson, "Parental Behavior May Increase Risk of Psychiatric Disorders in Children," Arch Gen Psychiatry, 58: 453–460.

3. Susan Taylor, *In the Spirit: The Inspirational Writings of Susan L. Taylor* (New York: Amistad, 1993), p. 85.

4. Alvin Poussaint & Amy Alexander, *Lay My Burden Down* (Boston: Beacon Press, 2000), p. 96.

5. Carolyn Wesson, *Women Who Shop Too Much* (New York: St. Martin's Press, 1990), p. 9.

6. Frantz Fanon, *Black Skins, White Masks* (Boston: Grove Press 1967), p. 25.

7. John W James & and Frank Cherry: *The Grief Recovery Handbook: A Step-by-Step Program for Moving Beyond Loss* (New York: Harper Perennial, 1988), p. 23.

8. Kris L. Easton, Cynthia Russell, & Jack Birge, *Congregational Health: How to Make Your Church a Health-aware Community* (Roscoe, Il, 2002).

9. Kevin W Cosby, *Finding God* (Louisville: Christopher Publications, 1995), p. 14.

10. Linda Hollies, *Inner Healing for Broken Vessels: Seven Steps to a Woman's Way of Healing* (Nashville: Upper Room Books, 1992, p. 15.

11. Jonetta Rose Barras, *Whatever Happened to Daddy's Little Girl? The Impact of Fatherlessness on Black American Women* (New York: The Ballantine Publishing Group, 2000), p. 212.

12. Mark Katz, *On Playing a Poor Hand Well* (New York: WW Norton & Company, 1997).

13. Emmy E Werner and Ruth S Smith: *Overcoming the Odds: High Risk Children from Birth to Adulthood.* Ithaca: Cornell University Press, 1992.

14. Gordon Allport, "Introduction," in Victor Frankel, *Man's Search for Meaning* (New York: Pocket Books, 1984), p. 3.

15. Silverstein, "Somatic Depression," American Journal of Psychiatry, 1999. 156: 480–482.

16. C Brown et al., "Clinical Presentations of Major Depression by African Americans and Whites in Primary Medical Care Practice." *Journal of Affective Disorders* 41: 181–191, 1996.

17. F. M. Baker et al: "Screening African Americans for the Presence of Depressive Symptoms: A Preliminary

Investigation." *Journal of Psychiatry and Neurology* 9: 127–132, 1996.

18. The symptoms throughout this chapter are excerpted from American Psychiatric Association. *Diagnostic and Statistical Manual of Mental Disorders,* 4th ed. (Washington D. C.: American Psychiatric Press, 1994).

19. See note 4.

20. Hans Selye, "History of the Stress Concept," in *Handbook of Stress: Theoretical and Clinical Aspects,* ed. Leo Goldberger, and Shlomo Breznitz (New York: The Free Press, 1993), p. 80.

21. George Edmond Smith, *Weight Loss for African American Women* (Roscoe, IL: Hilton Publishing Company, 2001).

22. Julia Boyd, *In the Company of My Sisters: Black Women and Self-Esteem* (New York: Penguin Group, 1993), p. 39.

23. Gail Elizabeth Wyatt, *Stolen Women: Reclaiming Our Sexuality, Taking Back Our Lives* (New York: John Wiley Sons, Inc., 1997).

24. Audrey B Chapman, *Getting Good Loving: How Black Men and Women Can Make Love Work.* (New York: Ballantine Books, 1995), p. 35.

25. Alex Haley, *Roots: The Saga of an American Family* (New York: Doubleday, 1976).

26. Harold S Kushner, *How Good Do We Have to Be? A New Understanding of Guilt and Forgiveness* (Boston: Little, Brown and Company, 1996), p. 38.

27. Debrena Jackson Gandy, *Sacred Pampering Principles: An African-American Woman's Guide to Self-Care and Inner Renewal* (Self-published, 1998).

28. Judith Viorst, *Necessary Losses.* (New York: Simon & Schuster, 1986), p. 179.

29. Cecilia Williams Bryant, *Kiamsha: A Spiritual Discipline for African-American Women* (Baltimore: Akosua Visions, 1991), p. 135.

30. Maya Angelou, *I Know Why the Caged Bird Sings* New York (Bantam Books, 1971).

31. Bonnie St. John Deane, *Succeeding Sane: Making Room for Joy in a Crazy World*(New York: Simon & Schuster, 1998), p. 49.

32. Jawanza Kunjufu,*The Power, Passion, and Pain of Black Love* Chicago: African American Images, 1993) p. 103.

33. M. Scott Peck, *The Road Less Traveled: A New Psychology of Love, Traditional Values and Spiritual Growth* (New York: Simon & Schuster, 1978), p. 81.

34. Kahlil Gibran, *The Prophet* (New York: Alfred A. Knopf, 1923), p. 11.

35. Willie Hamlin, *The Chains of Psychological Slavery: The Mental Illness of Racism.* (Silver Spring: The Institute for Child and Family Psychiatry, Inc.), 1979.

36. Fanon, *Black Skins, White Masks.* See n. 6 above.

37. W. E. Cross, Jr., in *Black and White Racial identity: Theory, Research and Practice* (Westport, Ct.: Praeger, 1993), p. 20.

38. William Grier and Price Cobbs, *The Jesus Bag* (New York: McGraw-Hill Book Company, 1971)

39. Renita Weems, "Reading Her Way Through the Struggle: African-American Women in the Bible," in *Stony the Road We Trod: African American Biblical Interpretation, ed.* Cain Hope Felder (Minneapolis: Fortress Press, 1991), P. 66.

40. Randolph C. Byrd, "Positive Therapeutic Effects of Intercessory Prayer in a Coronary Care Unit Population," *Southern Medical Journal* 81: 826–829, 1988.

41. Balamani, Michele, inn *The Voice of Baraka* (Largo, MD: Baraka Counseling Center, n.d.

42. Kenneth Pargament, "Religion and the Problem-Solving Process: Three Styles of Coping," in *Journal for the Scientific Study of Religion.* 27: 90–104, 1988.

43. H.C. Meserve, "How Religion Heals." *Journal of Religion and Health* 20: 259–263, 1981.

Select Bibliography

Angelou, Maya, *I Know Why the Caged Bird Sings*. New York: Bantam Books, 1969.

Balamani, Michele, "in *The Voice of Baraka. Largo, MD: Baraka Couunseliang Center, n.d.*

Barras, Jonetta Rose, *Whatever Happened to Daddy's Little Girl? The Impact of Fatherlessness on Black Women*. New York: The Ballantine Publishing Group, 2001.

Booth, Leo, *When God Becomes a Drug: Breaking the Chains of Religious Addiction and Abuse*. Los Angeles: Jeremy P. Tarcher, Inc., 1991.

Boyd, Julia A., *In the Company of my Sisters: Black Women and Self-Esteem*. New York: Penguin Books, 1993.

Bryant, Cecilia Williams, *Kiamsha: A Spiritual Discipline for African-American Women*. Baltimore: Akosua Visions, 1991.

Byrd, Randolph C., "Positive Therapeutic Effects of Intercessory Prayer in a Coronory Care Unit Population," in *Southern Medical Journal 81: 826–829, 1988.*

Chapman, Audrey B., *Getting Good Loving: How Black Men and Women Can Make Love Work*. New York: Ballantine Books, 1995.

Clark, Kenneth B. and Mamie Clark, "Racial Identification and Preference in Negro Children," in *Readings in Social Psychology,* ed. T. M. Newcomb & E. L. Hartley. New York: Henry Holt, 1947.

Cross, W. E., Jr., "Models of Pscychological Nigrescence," in *Journal of Black Psychology* 5(1), 13–31.

Deane, Bonnie St. John: Succeeding Sane: Making Room for Joy in a Crazy World. New York: Simon & Schuster, 1998

Fanon, Frantz, *Black Skins, White Masks*. Boston: Grove Press Reissue edition,1991.

Gandy, Debrena Jackson, *Sacred Pampering Principles: An African-American Woman's Guide to Self-Care and Inner Renewal*. New York: William Morrow and Company, Inc., 1997.

Gaston, Marilyn Hughes & Gayle K. Porter, *Prime Time: The African American Woman's Complete Guide to Midlife Health and Wellness*. New York: The Ballantine Publishing Group, 2001.

Gibran, Kahlil, *The Prophet. New York: Alfred A. Knopof, 1923*.

Grier, William & Price Cobbs, *The Jesus Bag*. New York: McGraw-Hill Book Company, 1971.

Haley, Alex: *Roots, The Saga of an American Family*. New York: Doubleday, 1976.

Hamlin, Willie, *The Chains of Psychological Slavery: The Mental Illness of Racism*. Silver Springs, Md: The Institute for Child and Family Psychiatry, Inc., 1979

Hooks, Bell, *All About Love*. New York: Harper Collins, 2000.

Hopson, Derek, and Darlene Powell-Hopson, *Different and Wonderful: Raising Black Children in a Race-Conscious Society.* New York: Prentice Hall, 1990.

Hull, Akasha Gloria, *The New Spirituality of African-American Women.* Rochester, Vermont: Inner Traditions International, 2001.

Kaufer, Nelly, and Carol Osmer-Newhouse, *A Woman's Guide to Spiritual Renewal.* New York: Harper Collins, 1994.

Kunjufu, Jawanza, *The Power, Passion and Pain of Black Love.* Chicago: African American Images, 1993.

Kushner, Harold S., *How Good Do We Have to Be? A New Understanding of Guilt and Forgiveness.* Boston: Little Brown and Company, 1996.

LaBelle, Patti, *Don't Block the Blessing.* New York: Riverhead Books, 1996.

Lightner, Ann Farrar, *And Your Daughters Shall Preach: Developing a Female Mentoring Program in the African-American Church.* St. Louis: Hodale Press, Inc., 1995.

Meri Nana-Ama Danquah: *Willow Weep for Me.* New York: W W Norton & Company, 1998.

Morrison, Toni, *The Bluest Eye.* New York: Alfred A. Knopf, 1970.

Peck, M. Scott, *The Road Less Traveled: A New Psychology of Love, Traditional Values and Spiritual Growth..* New York: Simon & Schuster, 1978.

Phillips, Crystal, *The Me I Knew I Could Be.* New York: St Martin's Press, 2001.

Richardson, Brenda, and Brenda Wade, *What Mama Couldn't Tell Us About Love.* New York: HarperCollins, 1999.

Smith, George Edmond: Weight Loss for African American Women. Roscoe, Il: Hilton Publishing Company, 2001.

Viorst, Judith, *Necessary Losses*. New York: Simon & Schuster, 1986.

Weems, Renita, "Reading Her Way Through the Struggle: African-American Women in the Bible," in *Stony the Road We Trod: African-American Biblical Interpretation,* ed. Cain Hope Felder. Minneapolis: Fortress Press, 1991.

Wyatt, Gail Elizabeth, *Stolen Women: Reclaiming Our Sexuality, Taking Back Our Lives*. New York: John Wiley & Sons, Inc., 1997.

Index

ABC's of mental health, 181–195
acceptance of oneself, 12,
    141–142
adulthood, emotional problems
    carried over from childhood,
    9–10
    healing childhood wounds,
    46–48
adversity, reading inspiring
    books to overcome,
    148–149
African American women
    abilities needed to be effective
        individual, 10–11
    and fear of success, 52
    image in the media and,
        106–107
    myths about, 61–62
    and poor mental health,
        explanation for, 19–21
    "superwoman", myth of being
        a, 31, 86–87, 111

African Americans
    negative stereotypes, 112
    positive attitude about iden-
        tity, developing a, 163–166
    rich heritage, learning about,
        112–113
aggressive behavior
    as coping strategy, 31–32
    stifling, 106
alternative medications. See also
    medications
anger. See racism
anorexia nervosa (eating disor-
    der), 74
anti-anxiety medications,
    132–133
anti-depressants, 129–131
anti-psychotics (major tranquil-
    izers), 131–132
anxiety disorders, 68–74
    acute stress disorder, 71
    medications for, 132–133

panic disorder, 69–70

personal narrative, 68

Post Traumatic Stress Disorder (PTSD), 71

Aesop's Fable, "The Wonderful Tar Baby Story", 43

attention-deficit/hyperactivity, 79

bibliography, 203–206. *See also* books

bipolar disorder (manic-depressive illness), 65–66

anti-manic medications, 133–134

symptoms of, 66

blind loyalty, to family and past, 34–36

books (recommended reading), 22, 38, 57, 84, 101, 113, 138, 154–155, 167, 178

breathing exercises, for stress relief, 95–96

bulimia nervosa (eating disorder), 75

change, living with, 53–56

childhood sexual abuse, 109–110

impact on adult relationships, 151–152

personal narrative, 139–140, 153–154

childhood

emotional problems influencing adult behavior, 9–10

overcoming abusive, 51–52, 109–110

pseudo-independence, being raised with, 111–112

chronic pain, and depression, 62

church, importance of, 170–171

cognitive behavioral treatment, for stress relief, 135–136

control, what is and what is not, 13–14

coping strategies, 11–12

example of, 30–31

glossary of terms, 26–30

denial, defined, 27

dependence disorders, 78–79

dependency, and African American women, 110–112

depression, 4, 60–67

bi-polar disorder and, 65–66

diabetes and, 67–68

dysthymic disorder, 66

elderly and, 61

exercise, as treatment for, 135

factors contributing to, 64

hormones and, 64

medications, 128–134

and parenting, effect on, 9

personal narratives, 7–8, 21–22, 59–60, 83

postpartum depression, 66

seasonal affective disorder, 67

somatic depression, 64

statistics on, 4

and suicide, 75–77

symptoms, 60–61, 65

checklist, 63

physical, 62–64

women and, 61

diabetes, and depression, 67–68

disappointments, exercise to
    help deal with, 54–55
disassociation, defined, 28
displacement, defined, 27
Douglass, Frederick, quote on
    raising children, 9
dreams and hopes, 41–42
    exercise to help fulfill expecta-
        tions, 42, 54–55
drugs. *See* medications
dysthymic disorder, and depres-
    sion, 66

eating disorders, 74–75
    anorexia nervosa, 74
    bulima nervosa, 75
emotional patterns, strong hold
    of, 24–25
exercise, physical
    for depression treatment, 135
    for stress relief, 97–99

failure, exercise to help overcome
    fear of, 50
family connection, 15–17. *See also*
    parenting
    blind loyalty to, 34–36
    emotional patterns, rooted in
        childhood, 24–26
    family therapy, 136
    marital therapy, 136–137
fear
    difference between anxiety
        and, 69
    of failure, exercise to help
        overcome, 50
friendships. *See also* relationships
    between women, 146–148

types of, 145
fronting, (psychological term),
    46, 87
future, looking towards a posi-
    tive, 179–181

gambling addiction, 78
glossary of psychological terms,
    26–30
God, belief in. *See also* spirituality
    role in mental health and,
        172–174
    using presence as coping style,
        174–177
grief and loss, 14, 40–49, 57
    coming to terms with, 42–44
    grief process, 45–46
    learning how to grieve, 42–46
    personal narrative, 39–40, 56
    re-parenting yourself, 46–49
    successful grieving, 42–46,
        88
    unfinished business, coping
        with, 44–45

healing process, exercise to help
    with, 54–55
hormones, and depression, 64

identification (psychological
    term), defined, 28
    with the aggressor, 28–29
impulse-control disorder, 77–78
intellectualization, defined, 29
intermittent explosive disorder,
    78
isolation (psychological term),
    defined, 29

journal, keeping a
    exercise to help with grief
        process, 46
    spiritual exercise, 177
    for stress relief, 88–89
    for stress screening, 89–90
joy, ability to experience, 13

kleptomania, 78

labyrinth walk (type of medita-
    tion), 99–100
learning disorders, 79
life management plan
    developing a, 85–101
    stress screen and, 89–90
life's challenges, managing, 12
loss. *See* grief and loss
love
    relationships and, 149–152
    self-love, importance of,
        140–142, 143

manic-depressive illness. *See*
    bipolar disorder
medications, 18, 128–134
    alternative/natural, 134
    anti-anxiety, 132–133
    anti-depressants, 129–131
    anti-manic, 133–134
    anti-psychotics, 131–132
    doctor's caution regarding,
        128–129
medicine. *See* medications
meditation, for stress relief,
        96–97
    technique, 96–97
    walking meditation, 99–100

mental disorders, 77–82. *See also*
    depression
    impact on family, 81–82
    medical condition causing,
        67–68
    medications, 128–134
    personal narrative, 59–60
    treatments without medica-
        tions, 134–137
    when help is needed, 79–83
mental health
    ABC's of, 181–195
    African American women and,
        3, 8
    defined, 8–9
    inventory, 5
    meaning of, 12–21
    poor, explanation for, 19–21
    resistance to seeking help, 35
    risk factors contributing to
        poor, 19–20
    statistics on, 20
    steps to optimum, 22, 37–38,
        56–57, 100, 113, 138, 154,
        167, 178
mental health professionals,
        120–127
    choosing a therapist, 124–125
    female African American ther-
        apists, 124
    overcoming mistrust of,
        17–19
    seeking help from, 36
    survey results on therapists,
        126–127
    treatments provided by,
        120–123
mental health services, 117–124.

See also treatments for mental
  health disorders
aftercare, 80
fear of seeking treatment,
  82–83
finding care, 119–123
finding money to pay for, 120
keys to good, 49
interventions, types of,
  118–119
involuntary commitments,
  123–124
personal narrative, 117
psychiatric admissions, 80
seeking help from, 79–83
mistrust, problem of, 17–19
movies recommended, 22, 38,
  57, 84, 101, 113, 138, 155,
  167, 178

natural medications, 134. *See also*
  medications
nurturing, positive effects of,
  25–26, 153

obesity, 74
obsessive-compulsive disorder,
  70

panic attack, 68–69
panic disorders, 69–70
  medications for, 133
  personal narrative, 83
parenting. *See also* family connection
  good, 10, 152–153
  raising strong children, 49–51
  re-parenting yourself, 46–49

past
  having blind loyalty to, 34–36
  learning to deal with the,
    14
personal narratives
  childhood sexual abuse
    (Aleshya), 139–140,
    153–154
  depression
    (Brenda), 7–8, 21–22
    (Yolanda), 59–60, 83
  depression and suicide
    (Tonya), 85–86, 100
  grief and loss (Darlene),
    39–40, 56
  panic disorder (Sheila), 83
  positive outlook (Phyllis),
    179–180
  psychotic disorder (Tiffany),
    72, 83–84
  racism (Nicole), 157–158,
    164–166
  reckless behavior (Sharon),
    33–34
  seeking mental health treat-
    ment (Lorraine), 117,
    137–138
  self-esteem (Valerie), 103–104,
    113
  shopping addiction
    (Stephanie), 23–24, 33, 37
  spirituality, role of (Linda),
    169–170, 177–178
phobias, 70
  obsessive-compulsive disor-
    der, 70
  social, 70
  specific, 70

physical well-being, maintaining, 15, 36
pleasure, ability to experience, 13
Post Traumatic Stress Disorder (PTSD), 71
postpartum depression, 66
prejudice. *See* racism
projection (psychological term), 28
proverbs, African, 35, 46
psychiatrists. *See* mental health professionals
psychologists. *See* mental health professionals
psychosis, 72–73
psychotic disorders, 72–74
    involuntary commitments, 123–124
    medications for, 132–133
    personal narrative, 72, 83–84
    psychosis, 72–73
    schizophrenia, 73–74
pyromania, 78

racism, 157–167
    anger, letting go of, 161–163
    effect on mental health and, 19
    legacy of, 36
    personal narrative, 157–158, 164–155
    positive Black identity, developing, 163–166
    prejudice, how it comes about, 158–161
rationalization (psychological term), 28
re-parenting yourself, 46–49

reaction formation (psychological term), 29
regression (psychological term), 30
relationships, 142–153
    difficulties in forming, 142–145
    childhood sexual abuse, 151–152
    different values , 149–151
    female friends, 146–148
    friendships, 145–149
    interpersonal, 14
    parent/child, 152–153
    partner, finding a, 149–152
    power of love, 150–151
    reading books as therapeutic measure, 148
religion, role in promoting mental health, 170–177
repression (psychological term), 27
resources. *See also* books; movies
    National Mental Health Association, 36, 84
    suicide prevention, 36

"saving our last nerve", taking to heart, 88–89
schizophrenia, 73–74, 119
seasonal affective disorder, 67, 135
self-acceptance, 12, 141–142
self-esteem, 114–115
    African American women and, 104–108
    healthy, 104